FEELING THE HEAT

AN INTERROGATION
OF THE SOUL

By John P. Contini

1/7/08

Carl +
Carole

you two have been
so kind & encouraging to
me. May God
bless you & your
family, beyond all
measure! a friend,
JP Contini

Jere:
29:11

Author's Web Sites

www.JPContini.com
www.LibertyPressPublishing.com
www.DangerRoadTheBook.com
myspace.com/jpcontinibooks

Individual copies: 1.800.957.6476

FEELING THE HEAT
AN INTERROGATION
OF THE SOUL

By John P. Contini

FEELING THE HEAT
AN INTERROGATION
OF THE SOUL

By John P. Contini

Feeling the Heat
copyright © 2008 John P. Contini

Printed in the United States of America
First Edition: Spring 2008
10 9 8 7 6 5 4 3 2 1

ISBN-13: 978-0-9773174-2-4
ISBN-10: 0-9773174-2-0

Liberty
PRESS

Cover design by Jeff Tidwell

Acknowledgements

First and foremost, I would like to give thanks to our Heavenly Father for all of His countless blessings, and to Jesus Christ, my Savior, and to the Holy Spirit, who provides me with limitless help and inspiration.

I would also like to thank...

Elizabeth, my sweet-spirited, Proverbs 31 wife, for putting up with me. No husband in the history of marriage has ever had a sweeter or more wonderful wife!

My three incredible children, *Kathleen*, 17, *Johnny*, 16, and *Mary*, 11, for bringing immeasurable joy, meaning and purpose to my life.

Don E. Contini, for teaching me how to be a man by his awesome example, and for being the world's greatest Pop.

Noreen Leahy, for teaching me by her own unparalleled example, how to love; and for inspiring me to write, and for otherwise being the world's best Mom!

Kathleen Contini Borres, my wonderful sister, for loving me unconditionally and for being one of the best human beings in the history of this planet.

Don R. Contini and *Anthony M. Contini* for being the world's best brothers. Each of my brothers are, by nature, more decent and kind than I am. They have helped me, by their examples, to be a better person.

Jeff Tidwell of *Homeward Media*, for going the Matthew 5:41 "extra mile" on his phenomenal cover design for FEELING THE HEAT — and also for his design of www.DangerRoadTheBook.com. There is nobody more responsive and more efficient than Jeff Tidwell.

Janice Valvano, my awesome editor, whom I owe a special debt of gratitude. Without her extraordinary help, this book would not have happened.

Anita Mitchell, Senior Editor of *Liberty Press Publishing*, for her tireless efforts at the helm of Liberty's publishing and grass roots success to date.

Martha Blumel of *Envision Graphic Design*, one of my incredibly gifted editors and graphic artists — whose consistent help was instrumental in bringing this book to life!

Howard Finkelstein, Broward Public Defender and WSVN/Channel 7's "Help me Howard," *Circuit Judge Robert Fogan*, Chief homicide prosecutor *Brian Cavanagh, Mike Dutko, Circuit Judge Paul Backman*, Detective Sergeant *Frank Miller* and *Pastor Jerome Dukes*, for simply being themselves and doing what they do best. I cannot thank these men enough for their friendship, loyalty and selflessness.

Chuck Prince, Alan Burnstein, Reed Tolber, Bob Stone, Howard Finkelstein, Jay York, Jeff Levy, Al Schreiber, Randy Goldberg, Kurt Kotrady, John Beach, Sal Verini and *H. Dohn Williams Jr.* — some of the best men I know. Some of these men are law enforcement officers of integrity, while others are some of the best trial lawyers in the business! These men have read and publicly recommended my first book, "DANGER ROAD: A true crime story of murder and redemption," and were that not enough … they each repeatedly encouraged me to continue writing, which culminated in the completion of this second book, "FEELING THE HEAT... an interrogation of the soul." Magistrates *Mindy Brown* and *Debbie McCloskey*, for their unwavering support and encouragement. They have each trumpeted the redemption message and success of the books to date, consistently encouraging me to keep on writing!"

Pastor David Blood, Ernie Johns, Mike Marcellino, Tony and *Christine Ferrara* and *Chaplain Freddie Guzman*, for their helpful and selfless prison distribution and ministry activities in getting the books to the Florida inmates.

Phil Lowry (owner and also a pastor!) and *Wes Jolly* of *Express Logistics*, the fulfillment center in Glasgow, Kentucky, for also going that extra mile in shipping FEELING THE HEAT to the folks who order the book through www.DangerRoadTheBook.com.

Chris Herridge and his awesome staff at *Telelink Call Center*, St. John's, Newfoundland, for always being so helpful with the callers who order FEELING THE HEAT via 1.800.957.6476.

Pastor Larry Thompson of *First Baptist Church* of downtown Fort Lauderdale, for being a wonderful man and pastor, and for also causing DANGER ROAD and FEELING THE HEAT to be sold and promoted at First Baptist's "Family Books & Music," its popular downtown bookstore; additional special thanks to *John* and *Shari Jones*, Music Ministers and worship leaders at First Baptist, for their friendship, encouragement and support during this project.

Pastor Derrick Gillis of *Zoe-Life*, for extending his pulpit to me on Father's Day and allowing me the coveted privilege of sharing the gospel message of redemption and forgiveness with his church.

Reverend Dave Blood and *Pastor Bob Sands*, for allowing me the special honor and privilege of sharing the Gospel from their respective pulpits at *New Hope Christian Fellowship* in Port Charlotte, Florida and *Community Bible Church* (Formerly Griffin Road Baptist Church) in Dania Beach, Florida.

Bob D'Andrea and *Stephanie O'Neal* of *Christian Television Network* (CTN) and its nationally renowned show, "The Good Life with Bob D'Andrea," for our sweet-spirited, nationally televised interview.

Janice Valvano, Laurie Quinn, Mimi Hiller, Kristin Egan and host *Joe Watkins* of *Trinity Broadcasting Network* (TBN), for inviting me on several occasions to be a guest on "Praise the Lord," TBN's internationally televised show and also on locally-televised "Joy in Our Town."

Dr. Ed Aqua of *Nova Southeastern University*, for his generosity in inviting me to speak to the undergraduate students, law school students and faculty at Nova Southeastern University and its prestigious law school.

Ernie Johns, for his selfless efforts in representing the books throughout Florida and the southern states.

Matt Nicolopoulos and *Johnny McLaughlin,* for their unwavering loyalty and friendship. Together with Johnny's wife *Patty*, they were there for me yet again throughout the difficult days in Atlanta.

Starbucks "Blend"

"Feeling the Heat, An interrogation of the soul," is a special 'blend' with Starbucks coffee — actually Starbucks Coffee Company, insofar as the book was written at Starbucks! To be exact, the T Mobile Hotspot at five different Starbucks stores in Broward allowed me to go wireless on my laptop and write the book whenever I had the right moments or thoughts in whatever part of the county I happened to be at that time. Starbucks was my "third place," as it's affectionately referred to within the company — away from home and the office, proving that anybody can write a book and get away for a cup of coffee at the same time! I will always believe that everyone has a book in them; it's finding the time to write it that's the challenge. *Artie Dohler*, the District Manager of Starbucks, and the following Starbucks store Managers were especially hospitable and inviting, even to the point of extending me the privilege of having some very special and fun book readings and booksignings once FEELING THE HEAT was published. These wonderful people are now my friends: *Paul Baker*, at the Broward and Federal store, *Jeff Neer*, at the Weston Town Center store, *Vionette Torres*, at the store across from The Galleria and *Lori Maron*, at the Flamingo Road store in Pembroke Pines.

Dedication

This book is dedicated to Rocco Contini, my uncle. He was the family patriarch who was loved by everyone. And he was the first person I went to for help. When I could not tell anyone of my plight — what is now revealed in this true story — I could tell *him*. He was strong; and yet he was always safe, because he always cared.

Contents

Chapter 1

Who's Playing Who?

"You OK?" Dutko asked.

Mike Dutko was an old friend of mine, another successful criminal defense lawyer in town. We used to hang out together years ago when we were both prosecutors. In fact, we shared a desk together, with Mike on one side and me on the other. Apparently, the crime problem in town was growing faster than the office's ability to keep up.

Dutko looked the part, almost like a cross between a Ben Affleck or George Clooney, with Spartacus. Then throw a suit on him, shades and an earpiece, put him outside one of the courthouses and he'd look like he was guarding the President. He once worked as an undercover narcotics cop with the Fort Lauderdale Police Department. With his chiseled beard and intimidating looks, he could obviously play the part of a drug dealer too.

Right out of law school, Mike married Betty and had three children in a row, becoming the quintessential family man, too straight for most of us. I used to nurse my hangovers and read the Sunday paper around his pool and have dinner with his family on an occasional Sunday, whenever I needed my fix of normalcy and family values after a couple of hard weekend nights out.

Mike was walking toward me in the courthouse hallway and must've noticed the worried look on my face.

I managed to mutter something while lifting my head.

"What's wrong?" Mike probed, appearing genuinely concerned.

"I think I'm in trouble, Mike."

"What kind of trouble?"

Before I could answer, he saw that I was having some

difficulty and was starting to get emotional, so he interrupted my thoughts.

"I'm heading back to my office. You want to come with me and tell me about it?"

I remember feeling relieved that I could finally tell someone what was torturing me. I had only shared my plight and my fears with my wife, my uncle Rocco and my father, and telling them didn't help at all. Their hearts were right, but they just made me answer too many naïve questions about the system — and besides, they weren't equipped at all to help me deal with the federal prosecutors and DEA agents assigned to the involved money laundering task force. I needed a real lawyer — a veteran like me, a veteran grounded with objectivity who would understand what I was going through and be in a position to help me.

I told him only half-truths, something he was used to. Our clients almost always tell us some of the truth sprinkled with some fiction, so I just gave him what my clients give me, more of the same.

Because Dutko did what I did for a living, he was used to getting half-truths. I almost felt a little guilty about playing him like this, but then I remembered that Mike had been an undercover narcotics cop who deceived people for a living.

Friend or no friend, why should I feel guilty about withholding truth from a guy who withheld the truth from almost everyone he met — and besides, I rationalized my deception by telling myself that I was only protecting him from an ethical dilemma.

But the Holy Spirit was still convicting me for being dishonest, so I changed channels in my mind. I got back to thinking about his own deception — how he would withhold the real facts and truth from countless people he'd "befriend" at bars, only to then arrest them after he had gained their confidence.

I told myself, "It takes a certain kind of person to do that. No, I have no guilt." And so I locked into that position, telling myself over and over again, that I had no guilt getting over on him, adding "facts" that never happened, withholding some that did.

We weren't in Dutko's office more than 15 minutes before I allowed myself to cry in front of him, prompting him to call Dr. Martin Brandon*, the famed forensic psychologist in town. Dutko did what *I* would have done, picking up the receiver and punching in Brandon's number without needing his client's permission. He was going to help me his own way, come hell or high water.

Here's where the confusion begins. I was manipulating Dutko, using him to effectuate my purposes — my hidden agenda *to get out of town*. But Dutko thought *he* was working *me*, getting me the help *he* knew I really needed. I knew what I was doing; I was embellishing my symptoms and letting the tears flow when I could've stopped them, and of course I knew he'd pick one of our forensic doctor friends to say what we'd expect he'd say — specifying that I had some particular diagnosis, just the sort of mental health defense I'd typically orchestrate for my own clients!

All of them — Dutko, my wife, Dr. Brandon and then two other forensic docs I had hired, apparently thought — or so they'd say — that I was missing a few lights from my chandelier that day, or my elevator wasn't stopping at every floor. Maybe I did too good a job in getting over on 'em, or perhaps they were just complicit with me in going along with my little Machiavellian machinations. I'd never know for sure whether they said what they said with a wink and a nod, but in either case, they were essentially putting a bow on my clever little mental health defense.

Whether they believed my disingenuous orchestrations or not, they wrote it up like I was Jack Nicholson in "Cuckoo's

* *This name was changed to protect his privacy.*

Nest." And if they were forced to say whether they were sincere in diagnosing me the way they did, they'd probably err on the side of self-preservation and say they believed in what they were saying and doing.

In fairness to Doc Brandon, he's the best in the business and that's why I always used him for my own clients. I thought Dutko would call him, but I knew I couldn't tell the truth to the doc about my embellishments. Like Dutko, he was way too straight to play the game. Maybe I did do too great an acting job, and *that's* what I should have been in life — an actor. Come to think of it, how else could I have won those high profile murder cases? It was easy to make myself cry in front of those people, which only convinced those juries that I believed in all I was selling!

Regardless of the real deal, within 30 minutes Doc Brandon was driving me to the institution de jour, "The Retreat" in western Broward County. The plan was for me to "detox" and be evaluated at The Retreat, before getting shipped outa dodge.

But as we pulled up to the facility and it looked like I was pulling it off, I panicked and almost backed out entirely.

"Doc, I can't do this thing after all. My kids are gonna think their daddy's a nut-job, and what about my business, the clients, our friends around the courthouse — I'll never live this down."

"John, you don't really have a choice anymore. You need a break, to get some rest. You're not sleeping. You said it yourself. There's no question that you're severely depressed; it's acute in my opinion, and you're only going to make it worse by trying to handle this thing alone and function like everything's normal.

"Give yourself a break. Do you know how many of your colleagues — judges we both know, big time lawyers in this town, and other forensic docs too — have gone through what you're going through? They've gone this exact same route. In fact, it's the thing to do in Hollywood anymore, didn't you know?"

Brandon was making me feel better as he parked close to the front door.

"But I don't have any other clothes or anything for staying here," I sheepishly replied.

"I'll call your wife and she'll bring you what you need, OK? That's what everybody does. Relax, John. It's going to be OK. It's all part of the process."

He then smiled, moved his head in the direction of the door with a sideways jerk, joking about how he wished that he could stay there for a few days to get away from it all. I remember him walking with his hand on my shoulder and gently directing us toward the entrance. A resignation of sorts came over me again, almost like the feeling I had when Dutko invited me back to his office.

Everything was cool till the woman told me to take off my belt and jewelry, apparently to inventory my belongings.

"Why the belt?" I nervously asked.

"Suicide is something we have to concern ourselves with here," she answered matter-of-factly.

"Hey, if I hang anyone it'll be you, not me sweetheart," I recall muttering.

With an edge in her voice, she inquired, "What did you say, Sir?"

"Nothing, I'm just talking to myself, I'm nuts, remember. That's what nut-jobs do, talk to themselves, right?"

She didn't look at all amused. "Maybe I should've taken that Dale Carnegie course after all," I thought.

Chapter 2

Outa Dodge; Into Atlanta

Before you could say "outa dodge," I was on a plane, headed for Atlanta.

"Remember, honey, you told me that some of your relatives were alcoholics, so it must run in *your* family," Elizabeth said. "You know I have it in *my* family too, so I'm not saying anything about your family that I'm not saying about my own, OK? I love you and I'm proud of you for what you're doing now, and I know you're doing it for us too," my wife continued.

All I could do was nod my head in quiet agreement as Elizabeth spoke. I was headed to a treatment center in Atlanta and was feeling lower than pond scum.

"Sir, may I bring you a beverage or a snack?" asked the flight attendant, oblivious to the fact that I, too, was oblivious.

"No thank you, we're okay," Elizabeth answered for both of us.

"Ladies and gentlemen, the seat belt sign has been removed. You are free to move about the cabin," announced the pilot, as I buried my face against the window.

"I believe this is a Godsend, John, to stop what you already know the Bible calls a generational curse. For three or four generations, I think it says, the sins of a father are passed down — you're doing a wonderful thing for our children, honey, so things will be different for them."

She was holding my hand now, leaning over and looking into my tired face, speaking with genuine sincerity. "Remember, God doesn't waste pain," she continued.

My wife was worried about me, and I felt guilty about that, but on another level she was happy that I was going to get the help she believed I needed. She and I both knew I'd been "self medicating" with too much red wine for the past few months, numbing my fear, anxiety, and depression.

As she was trying to comfort me, I thought to myself, "You of all people should know that I have legitimate reasons to be scared and depressed, so why are you buying all this crap from the docs about alcoholism?"

My mind took a vacation away from Elizabeth and the whole flight reality. She was saying something about our future, I recall, but I apparently chose not to hear her any longer. My forehead was braced against the window as my thoughts traveled down a darker and drearier memory lane. Time traveled back a few days even as we were traveling ahead at 500 mph. My eyes penetrated those clouds and fixed a stare that froze as long as my flashback. It was almost like a surreal time-warp into one of those "Back to the Future" movies, only my immediate past was way too real.

I flashed back to my client, Mike. We were to meet at the "Roasted Bean" coffee shop that is tucked away in a little strip of stores in Weston, the trendy upscale suburb in the western outskirts of Fort Lauderdale. Even before I walked into the coffee shop, I suspected something was wrong. The DEA agents hadn't called me back in a week. The federal prosecutor stopped returning my calls.

"Honey, are you OK?" asked Elizabeth, concerned about my lack of response.

I didn't hear her as I was too engrossed in the memory of the tortured days before my exodus.

The flight attendant handed her a blanket and pillow. "He may want these if he isn't feeling well," she suggested to Elizabeth.

I believe my wife covered me and placed the pillow by my head but I can't be sure.

For weeks I had been in almost daily communication with the DEA agents regarding my client, Mike, and his marijuana case. He was looking at a 10-year mandatory sentence, so he decided to do everything he could to cooperate with the government and get his sentence reduced.

"Whatever it takes," I recall him saying.

He essentially agreed to cooperate against his drug buddies, whether that meant wearing a wire and setting them up, engaging them in whatever incriminating conversations he could, testifying against them after they'd be indicted, anything to please the agents and the federal prosecutor.

Unfortunately, Mike's arrest was on the 11 o'clock news, and there was his mug all over television. Channel 7 showed him being carted off in handcuffs, so everyone in town knew he got busted. His drug buddies watched the news too, like everyone else, so they weren't doing business with him. When the DEA agents and the federal prosecutor stopped returning my calls, and when Mike started acting funny around me, something didn't pass the sniff test.

"Mike couldn't have turned on me," I thought, "because I already scored for him big time. My plea agreement with the Government provided for Mike to complete the "shock incarceration program" — a boot camp of sorts, and once he was done with that, he'd serve only 6 months in a federal "camp," the lowest level of security in the federal prison system. He should have been doing cartwheels and thanking God that he was *only* getting six months, instead of the original 10-year minimum mandatory prison sentence.

So then I thought, "He would never do *me* like that, or would he?"

Well built, sporting jeans, cowboy boots and his baseball cap worn backwards, Mike had that rough-and-tumble look of a Davie redneck. We sat in a couple of couch style chairs in the corner of the "Roasted Bean" coffee shop. He had a couple of cell phones in his possession — and it was that little detail that made me take notice, wake up and smell the coffee.

Mike was a contractor second, as it turns out, and *first* a hydroponics marijuana grower. Busted by the DEA and now prosecuted by the U.S. Attorney's Office, he was quite naturally afraid of going away for 10 years. In fairness to him, he had a four-year-old daughter, the same age as my little Mary. He was doing everything he could to weasel out of that mandatory minimum 10-year prison sentence to be with her, and I understood that.

He, like everyone else these days, was all about minimizing his own plight and working toward a lesser sentence. And apparently that included throwing his own lawyer under the bus!

"But he knew I was the sole provider for my three young children!" I screamed to myself on the plane. "He had been to my house many times. What he tried to do to me and my family is unforgivable," I angrily told myself.

I knew from all my years of representing guys who were cooperating with the police that you don't need to wear "body bugs" taped to your chest anymore like in the movies.

Today, law enforcement provides the confidential informant with what looks like a cell phone, but it's *really* a transmitter that's married to a UniTel listening device. Others look like beepers, but they're really not. These things I only learned from years of prosecuting and defending drug cases. They even have receivers, transmitters and other little gadgets they can put in baseball caps like the kind Mike wore.

Many of my own clients have been targeted by informants who wore all the latest and greatest, state-of-the-art undercover devices, so I've been privy to all kinds of knowledge that the feds don't like to share. For every client of mine on the wrong end of this covert equipment, I've had another actually wearing it.

I'm very friendly with a lot of local detectives and federal agents dating all the way back to my years as a Broward prosecutor. Though it's frowned upon, they even refer me business. If the DEA agents targeting me had been from Broward County, none of this would have happened. The Broward guys know the way I am, the way I do business.

I've represented so many cops who know I wouldn't have any interest whatsoever in a marijuana grow house; but these guys were DEA agents assigned to a money laundering task force out of Coral Gables in Miami-Dade County. They were young agents trying to nail a defense lawyer and get that coveted promotional notch in their belts.

"Honey, I'll be right back. I just have to use the restroom," Elizabeth assured me.

I still didn't hear her. I was hundreds of miles away in the "Roasted Bean" coffee shop, scared and fighting for our future.

Chapter 3

Targeting Your Lawyer

Something just didn't feel right when Mike sat across from me with those cell phones. He never carried more than one. Then he kept getting up to use the bathroom. I had been with him many times at the "Davie Grill" when he'd typically drink his huge cups of iced tea, and he had never gotten up repeatedly to use the bathroom like this. At the "Roasted Bean" that morning he got up to go twice within five minutes. That too wasn't right.

At the same time, I noticed way too much traffic in and out of the place. There were never more than three people at a time in this flunky little coffee shop where I'd hang out on occasion and hide from life as a lawyer. Now there were more than seven or eight men hanging out in pairs and pretending to be customers. These guys had apparently missed the "how to blend in" course at the academy, as they even looked like undercover cops. I'd been around way too many of them over 18 years as a former prosecutor and criminal defense lawyer, not to notice.

A four-door drove by the window too slowly. The front seat female passenger pretended to merely glance at me, but then she watched me for too long.

Months before the coffee shop scare, Mike's wife called me in a panic and cried to me about his arrest and federal indictment. The next morning I visited him in the holding cell at the Marshal's lock-up, and my old friend couldn't even make eye contact with me. He knew I'd be shocked to learn that he was a marijuana grower. He had conned me over time into believing that he was a small time contractor. In truth, even he'd have to admit that he was a wannabe builder who had simply been around long enough to know exactly where to find all the right subs for whatever needed doing by real working men.

He and his hung-over crew of flunkies performed all kinds of work for me in my office, anything from installing ceiling tiles and ceiling fans, to wood flooring and carpeting. They put up hurricane plywood at my house when I needed help, installed brick pavers around the pool, high hat light fixtures, you name it. I'm fairly useless at home with any of this do-it-yourself, Home Depot sort of thing, so maybe I looked the other way on what might have been fairly obvious to most defense lawyers.

His guys were always getting in trouble, mostly for DUI arrests and possession of marijuana; and then they would violate their probation by testing positive for drugs while on probation. Mike would then ask me to represent them and most times I did. He made sure I got paid. He took it out of their pay, and a lot of times I was paid in cash, or we worked out some sort of barter arrangement. They'd get to keep their liberty in exchange for which I'd get repairs and renovations done around my house and office. Fair enough.

They did decent enough work, and after work they'd go out and get trashed, I'm sure. They were kind of rough; frankly I thought it was a miracle they even showed up for work. They always tried to do a good job for me because they joked that they were going to need me again one day.

It seemed to me that Mike was doing well enough in his small time construction/repair business. He drove a shoulder height, fancy black truck — one of those diesel trucks with the huge wheels. He presented himself as a legitimate Davie redneck contractor; and truth be told, I remained clueless that he was also a marijuana grower.

To add insult to injury, I learned that his "construction" crew — my former clients — were also his marijuana grow house "do-boys," whose *main* tasks included watering, trimming and fertilizing the plants! They just happened to also know how to hurricane-proof the windows with the plywood, hang ceiling tiles and chair rail, and the whole nine yards.

The South Florida Money Laundering Task Force had been investigating my redneck "friend" and his marijuana grow-house operation for months. Just what I needed, I coincidentally had him and his minions in my house and office throughout the whole investigation; and as a consequence, I was included in their surveillance.

These feds were Miami DEA agents who didn't know me , so they had no reason not to think that I was dirty. In retrospect, I must have looked pretty slippery. The "legitimate" lawyer would normally meet his clients in his office, but not me: I was meeting these guys in coffee shops. Over the years we had become friends, so I'd sometimes meet Mike and his guys on my way to court at "Fried Green Tomatoes" or the "Davie Grill." We would talk about the work they were doing at my office or house, and I'd also get around to discussing their cases. Unbeknownst to me, our meetings were under surveillance the entire time.

To these agents, I must have looked like some Guido lawyer — with my Italian last name and my black Lincoln Town car (which looked too much like a limo) — when I met these guys out socially. It looked unprofessional, at a minimum, certainly without that healthy boundary of meeting in an office.

When the DEA ran a check on these little grow house "do-boys" and learned that they were each represented in the past by Contini, the same lawyer who was then representing Mike, their "boss," it had to appear as though I were a lawyer for the ring. How could it not look like I was facilitating that enterprise? It's fairly easy to look back and see how this would appear to law enforcement and understand why these agents were gunning for me.

But what I couldn't understand was why Mike, this big "tough" guy, wouldn't be man enough to go and do the six-month sentence standing on his head. The reason he shrunk to set me up was because he was "burnt" on the street. Nobody in his netherworld of dope dealing would do business with him. These clowns who doubled as agents went ahead and foolishly allowed his arrest to be filmed on TV. Their narcissistic need for press decimated any real chance he might have had to cooperate or perform what the prosecutors call "substantial assistance."

Muttering to myself, "He has no integrity, no character, no spine, no decency...."

"Pardon me?" Elizabeth asked.

"Nothing," I managed to say, before continuing the one-way conversation with myself.

"He's not at all the friend I thought he was. Why would anybody do that to a man who has three kids? I could understand if he was facing a 10-year sentence or if I, as his lawyer, had done *him* wrong, but I had already negotiated an awesome plea agreement in writing, signed by the Government! I got him all kinds of sweet results under the plea agreement — perks that most people would *never* get. I had him down to doing only six months at a minimum-security facility like Eglin Air Force Base or Maxwell Air Force Base, a virtual 'club fed.' It's a camp, not a real prison!"

Elizabeth was whispering something about how she loved me, and that was sweet, especially since we were hitting some real ugly turbulence.

My thoughts were just as turbulent. "This guy's going to a camp for only six months, and yet he won't even do that? He'd rather get me, his 'friend,' indicted and arrested and disgraced all over the newspapers, torn from my children, and sent to prison for *years*, than go to that camp for six months!"

My mind was racing faster than the engines on the plane.

My private conversation went uninterrupted for what seemed like forever as Elizabeth just periodically squeezed my hand. She knew I was miles away.

"What are you thinking about honey?" Elizabeth asked.

"These DEA agents want to nail me because I'm a lawyer. They see lawyers like me as big obstructionists in their lives. Law enforcement is in the business of arresting drug dealers and, in their view lawyers like me are raining on their parade by trying to get the bad guys off. They want to convict these dirt bags and they see us as equally dirty, just slippery suits trying to get these same dirt bags acquitted."

"John, it's not about them, honey; it's about *you* and getting *healthy.*"

"There you go again, thinking I'm a wackadoo who needs help with his addictions, some sort of paranoid nut job who's imagining all this crap about agents trying to get him. Come on, Elizabeth, this is *real*. I'm imagining nothing."

"Just try to rest, John."

Talking to the window and myself was easier. Nobody talked back that way. Bringing down a lawyer is kind of a trophy; the same goes for other professionals such as a judge or a doctor. Younger agents have a particular bent toward this, worse than veteran agents. By the time they're seasoned and older, they have a lot of lawyers as friends, and they're less judgmental. Younger DEA agents, right out of college or the academy, want to get a name for themselves. They want to look good to their supervisors. If they have a chance at getting a lawyer who they think is dirty, they're salivating like rabid dogs.

Even *before* the coffee shop meeting, I knew in my spirit that something was wrong. The paranoia was already setting in, so I contacted the federal prosecutor. I wanted to feel him out. He wouldn't return my calls, which only made it worse. I then called the agents. They wouldn't laugh and joke with me the way we did in the beginning. And that's a big part of the way I curry favor with agents and prosecutors. Getting them to like me and getting them laughing had always helped my clients. That's the way it started off with these guys, but it didn't stay that way.

My window view of the clouds was obscured again by the very real visual of the coffee shop. My mind permitted me no rest. All the "customers" in the "Roasted Bean," the two cell phones, Mike's repeated trips to the bathroom, the make and model of the car, its curious female passenger, the activity in the parking lot — *none* of this passed the sniff test. An inner warning in my spirit was delivering me yet again from a trap that was otherwise beautifully set.

Mike started bringing up things he had no business bringing up, asking me too many direct questions and talking about "cash" in the "old days," which frankly weren't that old. Instinctively, I went into a survival mode. I recall removing the battery from the back of one of his cell phones right in front of him, sticking it under a seat cushion. He looked confused and just quietly stared at me.

He was attempting to get me to acknowledge on the wire that I had received cash in amounts greater than $10,000. This was a critical figure, invoking certain federal statutory requirements. Receiving more than $10,000 in cash without filing the appropriate 8300 Form with the IRS can land someone in federal prison. If I had ever done anything like that — and of course I'd be a moron if I said I had — it would have been outside the time window of the otherwise applicable statute of limitations, to be sure — hence the "old days."

"John, you're just being paranoid," I remember saying to myself, but then he got up again to go to the bathroom. I would have bet he was in there using his other cell to call out for advice as to what to say or do. Regardless, I knew he was up to no good and I was scared.

When he brought up the "old days," I replied in broken sentences and used my fingers to reference certain numbers. This had to make me sound guilty as sin on audiotape, but thankfully there were no complete audible statements of an incriminating nature to hurt me — or so I hoped.

"What are you talking about, Mike, there was never any cash that I recall…."

He tried to get more words in, but I spoke over him, cutting him off very aggressively and preventing him from saying what he wanted. There was no question that I was bullying him in our "conversation" even though he's a big guy.

Repeating myself through his attempted interruptions, I continued, "We're friends, Mike. That's why I *never* charged you, and even though you paid me *no* money in this case…."

I was now in total survival mode, talking with my hands, talking about Christ and how Mike needed to come to church with me.

"Get this on the wire," was all I was thinking.

Whoever listened to that tape heard some of my favorite scriptures — those I was giving Mike. Every time he brought up "cash," I'd talk over or refute whatever he was trying to say. And I'd tell him of my hope and faith too — and how he too can have the same hope and faith, as I threw in a few of the best Bible verses I knew.

"You're such a fraud in the faith, John," I was now thinking in retrospect, staring into the clouds.

Elizabeth had left after telling me to rest, but she then returned to her seat and started rubbing my head, squeezing my hand. I recall feeling her love and support. It was comforting, so I leaned back off the glass window of the plane. She rubbed my forehead and stroked my hair too. I started feeling better.

But I was still stuck and broken down on memory lane. Back to torturing myself, my thoughts again turned to the agents, those preppie GI's. They'd consider everything I had aggressively said to Mike to be one big "false exculpatory," as they like to call it in prosecution circles. They call it a "false exculpatory" when a person knows that he or she is being targeted and surreptitiously recorded, choosing to say things on tape which are *knowingly* false, in order to muddy up the law enforcement wire. That's why law enforcement is careful to not blow their surveillance, so the target doesn't have the opportunity to create a false exculpatory.

They can call it whatever they want, but one thing's for certain: I was scared to death and making sure I got what *I* wanted on that wire. My spirit was screaming at me to get out of there.

"Run!" I thought, "But not before you run your mouth!"

Chapter 4

The Real Descent

I've been involved in enough of these operations in the past to know there were at least 10 to 14 agents and as many as six cars used for that surveillance and possible take down. They didn't appreciate my actions, which is why they showed up at my church the following morning. They would've dogged me everyday, had I not disappeared.

Just then the weight-challenged moron in front of me put his seat back like he owned the plane.

"What kind of idiot doesn't say 'pardon me' or 'excuse me' when they put their seat back in your face?" I asked the passing flight attendant loudly enough for Mr. Manners to hear.

His seat started to move forward a bit, as Elizabeth waved off the flight attendant.

"Honey, he doesn't know. Please relax sweetheart. Here, put your head down on my shoulder, and just close your eyes," Elizabeth added, putting out the new fire before I had a chance to rage. The silence was nice, though it didn't last.

"Like the doctors said, you're allergic to alcohol," she started again. "They're saying you have a biogenetic predisposition to alcoholism. You inherited those genes, so it's not your fault; but it *would* be your fault if you didn't do anything about it."

"But I'm not..." I started to say while lifting my head from her shoulder.

"You may not be an alcoholic *yet*," she interrupted. She had already anticipated my defense.

"But if you don't stop, John, you will probably *become* one, just like some of your relatives, my dad, and everyone else who comes from a family of heavy drinkers. I know you love our kids more than anything, so look at it this way; you're giving them a fresh start."

Elizabeth was on a roll now with this big pep talk on the plane.

"I hear you," is all I could mutter.

It started to help a little, if only to know that she was doing her level best to encourage me. It made me feel closer to her, that perhaps she loved me after all. But then I only felt guiltier, knowing that she was sincere and I wasn't. She was yet another victim of my manipulation. My depression only deepened as we approached Atlanta.

If anyone had told me a year earlier that I'd be going to a treatment center for addiction and recovery, I'd have told them they were smoking something funny.

"Ladies and Gentlemen, we are beginning our descent into Atlanta," announced the pilot. "Be careful when opening the overhead bins to retrieve your carry-on baggage as items may have shifted during the flight. Please remain in your seats until the seat belt signs are no longer illuminated."

Tuning the pilot out was easy as I went back to obsessively worrying about my family. My wife could handle this, I knew, as she was obviously very strong and still supportive; but I couldn't stop worrying about our kids, and I was scared for myself too.

"Kathleen and Johnny are only ten and nine, and Mary is only four!" I screamed inside my head. And to make matters worse, I was too scared to be honest with them.

It wasn't just unadulterated fear; the sin of pride was rearing its ugly head too. Emphasizing my need to protect the children from a consuming fear, I cautioned Elizabeth to only say, "Daddy is working on a big case in Atlanta," whenever they asked why I was gone. I didn't want the kids to worry about their daddy going to jail while they were getting ready to go to sleep for the night. It was bad enough that *I* had to think about it. Why not let them believe I had a case in Atlanta? It was true! Daddy had the biggest case ever there — his *own*!

"You're not protecting them, John," I argued with myself. "You're protecting yourself and your reputation with them. It's nothing but shame you're dealing with, and that ugly sin of pride."

But then the other John argued back just as convincingly as the protector of the children and their fragile and developing psyches, so I never knew the real truth as I got lost in both identities.

Elizabeth knew what I knew, and thankfully she didn't call me on it. She could see it on my face, and I could *see* that she could see it, so I turned back to the window.

Chapter 5
The Five P's

During our coffee shop conversation on Saturday, I had told Mike to meet me the next morning at my church at 10:30. He'd been there before when we invited him to our annual Christmas pageant, so he knew the church.

"Meet me and sit with me at the service at 10:30am, on the pew toward the back right side of the church, the right side as you're facing the preacher, the fourth pew from the back," I told him.

I wanted to study him more and know what he was up to, but the environment had to be safer.

"Was I making another mistake, asking him to join me at church?" I thought.

Then I remembered that line from the Godfather movie, "Keep your friends close and your enemies closer."

"Shame on you, John," I accused myself. "Sometimes you quote from the Bible and now you're quoting from the Godfather movie, as though they're equally authoritative, you moron!"

It was Easter Sunday and I'll never forget that day. My ten-year-old daughter Kathleen was wearing her beautiful new Easter dress and holding her matching little Easter bag.

Mike didn't show up like he said he would. Instead, two other guys showed up right where he and I agreed that he would sit. It was just as if someone had been listening to our conversation in the parking lot the day before and decided to mess with me.

They weren't dressed for church, or certainly not for a Southern Baptist church. Everyone else in attendance was dressed nicely, in their Sunday best. That's typical for any Sunday in this church, let alone Easter Sunday. They were undercover cops, no doubt.

It was so obvious. One guy was black, the other white; their shoes were too similar, and equally inappropriate; they wore jeans and zippered waist bags, the kind people wore in the 1980's that held their money, keys, cocaine and a convenient pistol. Both men, curiously enough, had a lot of earring holes. Anyone in my business for more than a few years could spot undercover cops, even on a bad day.

Halfway through the service, at the point when the preacher asked folks to shake hands with everybody around them, the two cops turned around and studied me *way* too long, while reluctantly shaking my hand. All around I could hear people saying, "Peace be with you" while they shook hands.

These two guys just kept looking at me, and I was scared to death. As God is my witness, I thought I was going to jail that morning. They were doing me a courtesy, I thought, by waiting until church was over, waiting until my kids weren't around, and for that much, I was almost thankful. But I was petrified. My future was gone. All I saw were the headlines of my arrest and the pain in my family.

"What are my children going to think?" I kept asking myself. "What will I tell my kids?"

As I imagined my imminent separation from my family, I started missing them beyond measure in spite of the fact that I hadn't even left the pew. Confronted with loneliness and fear, I prayed a lot during that service.

I had about two thousand in cash in my pocket, which I took out and put in my daughter's Easter bag. She had no clue why I told her to have Mommy empty her bag after church.

"Please go see Mommy in the nursery, OK? She is with Mary and watching the other kids too," I added anxiously to my daughter Kathleen.

I ushered her out because I didn't want her to see me get arrested. When the church service ended, the undercover guys left without a word. I went up to the pastor and told him how

I needed help and that I was in big trouble. He saw the emotion in my face. He did his best to console me. Then I went out to face the music. But they were gone, thank God.

Perhaps their presence at the Easter service was a warning, their way of saying: "You think you're a pretty slick dude, the way you talked and used your little hand signals at the coffee shop. You had an entire little private conversation without us being able to intercept anything intelligible, and we knew exactly what you were doing. And then you have the audacity to talk with your buddy about God and church. You think you're pretty slick, huh?"

When I finally realized that I wasn't going to be arrested on the spot, I felt relieved and wasted. That's when the plan for getting outa dodge was hatched. — for legal reasons. Frankly, I would've been happy going anywhere, even to a treatment center for people addicted to maple syrup or glue sniffing — *anything* to get out of town.

I was willing to jump through whatever legal hoops I had to jump through to guard against what I thought was my imminent federal indictment. The ominous and humiliating headlines had been repeatedly splashed across the big screen in my mind for days now, "Criminal defense lawyer arrested for money laundering…."

It was at this time that I conceived of this clever, albeit disingenuous, whole recovery thing. The street lawyer in me was working overtime as I went about the legal-beagle business of first *creating* and then *building* my "mental-health" defense.

"The five P's," I thought, "Prior planning prevents poor performance."

My preemption instincts kicked into overdrive as I kept busying myself in frightened preparation for that federal indictment.

Just then the airplane hit some real bumpy air and

seemingly dropped a couple hundred feet, not unlike an elevator free-falling a floor or two before getting right again. Passengers were too shocked to cry out; they just looked at each other when it was over, a few shaking their heads in obvious disapproval.

The pilot announced, "Ladies and gentlemen, please fasten your seatbelts as we are encountering some choppy air...."

"You call *that* choppy air?" I interrupted.

"Let's pray about our kids, John, and you'll feel better, OK?" suggested Elizabeth.

She always knew when we should pray. She was right; it did make me feel better. But my wife was still clueless on the real deal here, or she simply wouldn't buy what I was selling. She bought what these docs were telling her, hook, line and sinker.

"Hopefully," I thought, "the feds will buy it too, just like Elizabeth."

But then I asked myself, "Did I really fool her, or am I fooling *myself*? Am I *really* an alcoholic or addict?"

I settled on the fact that only God knew the *real* truth, and in the final analysis, only *He* could really help me with all this.

Chapter 6

One Flew Over the Cuckoo's Nest

Elizabeth escorted me through the doors into the lobby of the Talbott Recovery Campus, apparently sensing I needed her help. The old Jack Nicholson flick, "One Flew over the Cuckoo's Nest," was showing again on that screen in my head, except this was no movie!

Elizabeth asked, "What are you looking for, Honey?"

She had noticed me looking all around for Nurse Ratched, preparing myself for those saltpeter pills she'd be force-feeding me.

Then, I imagined I'd have to find a big enough guy like Chief — someone strong enough to throw the urinal through the front window, to get me out of there before my forced lobotomy!

"Sweetheart, we have to get you admitted over here," Elizabeth gently prodded, bringing me back from cuckoo's nest into reality.

Diane was the perfect greeter, her smile as sincere as her spirit. She was all blonde and yet personified the opposite of the characteristic stereotype, with a very kind and gentle affect. She wasn't provocative or even flirtatious, and yet she had our attention. Dressed beautifully and pretty in a sisterly sort of way, I'd soon learn that she was everyone's friend, always willing to say an encouraging word. Diane made me feel welcome and comfortable right away.

"Well hello, sweetie, come closer so I can shake your hand. I always like to be the first to welcome our new guests and tell you how much I admire what you're doing." She was just so genuine and warm, that I couldn't help but feel better almost immediately.

"Hi, I'm John, and we're checking in," I managed to

respond, shaking her hand. Her hand was as warm as her heart and that much was obvious to the touch.

"You'll enjoy it here, John, and we're gonna enjoy having you with us," Diane replied.

Elizabeth helped to make the introductions even smoother, making small talk about Diane's southern accent and the fact that they had both been raised in the south.

We weren't away from Diane for more than 10 seconds before the warmth had dissipated and I was feeling the chill of this dark reality once again. The admitting nurse's demeanor was in stark contrast to Diane's. She was more like Nurse Ratched than Miss Congeniality, with zero sensitivity to a man's hurting pride.

"Sir, we'll need you to drop a urine now. Here's your cup and you can use that bathroom there, while your wife is signing the admissions forms."

"Why don't I just drop my drawers here and bend over, sweet lips," I felt like telling this bimbo, but I didn't. My attitude sucked and I knew it. Instead, I just reached for my cup and shuffled over to the boy's room like the compliant dog that I was at that moment.

I almost wished there were narcotics in my urine when I reentered the room with my little plastic cup. Then all this madness would be worth it, and it would even make more sense; but instead, the only concern they'd get after analyzing my little specimen, would be its seemingly toxic levels of caffeine. There was so much caffeine in my system that my urine could probably be sold in remote parts of this world as the latest and strongest "organic espresso."

My wife and I exchanged big hugs in front of "Miss Urinalysis," as Elizabeth fought back her tears.

"Please make the most of this opportunity, John. I love you and the children adore you too. You're a great father and you're doing this for all of us, and I am so proud of you," she continued, as we hugged longer and tighter.

Wiping away her tears now, I found the strength and selflessness to say, "It's going to be great, Baby. I'll get healthy again and I'll be with you guys before you know it."

Miss Congeniality couldn't just sit there and let us do our thing. She decided to play Dr. Ruth and broker a few more tears.

"He will be a new man, Honey, and you two are going to have a better marriage, more fun and a brand new beginning when you see him again."

I wanted to smack her for stealing my moment with Elizabeth, and I suppose my look told her as much. She then morphed back into Nurse Ratched and disappeared underneath the mountain of paperwork she'd made us sign.

Chapter 7

Campus life

The Talbott Recovery Campus appeared like a college campus, only without the partying. There were coeds too, only they were off-limits like the drugs and alcohol. It wasn't cold and clinical like you might imagine when you think of a treatment center. The buildings were attractive and surrounded by aesthetically beautiful landscaping.

Everyone dressed nicely and spoke respectfully, regardless of whether they were staff or residents; in fact, it was next to impossible to differentiate the two. TRC was once exclusively reserved for addicted physicians, so it only made sense that most of the residents would be recovering docs who blended too easily with staff.

We had our choice of caffeinated or decaffeinated coffee throughout the day and early evenings, and we had unlimited access to the sweets from the candy bar machines. I got so addicted to these cellophane-wrapped Honey Buns that I thought about starting my own "Honey Bun support group."

Also like college, the schedule of meetings was arranged so that you could go from class to class, to the different groups — referring to the "process groups" and "primary groups." The process groups were designed to force you to "process" your issues among the other recovering addicts who would then provide "helpful" feedback.

If you didn't like their "feedback" and you threatened them — as I may or may not have done, depending on who's listening — you could get in trouble, like I did. Or you could lie in wait, as I often did, and give them equally hurtful "feedback" as they processed their own issues. Either way, counselors and therapists were present throughout each group to keep people like me honest and in line.

Love to Hate

The women were the most vicious with their highly negative and critical feedback, especially toward each other. A couple of them had even less love for me. Susan, one of the more critical women in my process group, loved to attack me. She seemed to get off even more in attacking my faith, as evidenced one morning by her particularly poignant accusation:

"Your *religion* didn't keep you out of here, Jesus boy."

"It's not a religion; it's a relationship," I recall telling her. "He knows that I am flawed and imperfect."

I should have quit while I was doing well enough with that retort, but I just had to keep running my mouth.

"If I could do this thing we call life without His help, He never would have had to go to the cross."

"You're such a hypocrite and a total jerk!"

Nanci Stockwell, our primary group therapist, put a stop to her verbal attack. Susan just contorted her hateful face and scowled at me, while the others in the group ignored both of us.

Then I retorted," Susan, it's not too late even for *you* to get right with Christ."

"That's enough you two," chided Nanci. "Someone else self-relate?" No one spoke up.

It worked; Susan hated me even more. But my satisfaction waned when I came under conviction for using His name as an instrument of division and war, instead of love and grace.

The group's assigned therapist would often need to interrupt and admonish the person giving the feedback, saying, "Remember — self relate," referring to the requirement that the feedback be about how *you*, as the person giving the feedback, have struggled with the *same* issue, and what you've learned about yourself. They didn't want other residents to play counselor or psychoanalyze others who were processing their issues.

Bedtime at drug camp

My first night I felt alone and dejected. The next night I listened to the Bible on tape and I felt better, so that became my nightly medicine for the remainder of my stay at TRC.

Listening to the tapes was easier for me than reading my Bible. I brought my Bible to drug camp as more of a good luck charm or a kind of security blanket. Many times I recall wishing that I was one of those guys who had that genuine depth of belief to actually open and read it.

"Please Lord, give me a real desire to read your word daily, to WANT to read the Bible, Father," I'd pray almost aloud.

I remember opening my Bible one night in my bed and reading the notes I had scribbled inside. My pastor had apparently said some pretty good stuff, as I had quotation marks around these handwritten notes:

"This is the instruction manual for your life. You have to pay careful attention to the instructions and then follow those instructions."

"Boy, easier said than done," I said out loud, forgetting for a moment that I wasn't alone.

Thankfully my remarks weren't audible enough to awaken my sleeping roommate. I glanced over again to see that he wasn't stirring. His snoring confirmed the obvious, allowing me to return to the scribbled notes in my Bible:

"This book was written by the One who designed and manufactured you."

"This instruction manual for your life — it's the ONLY book that not only teaches you how to live; it teaches you how to die."

"I'll be letting you teach me, Father, now that you've got my attention," I told myself.

It was then I remembered the old saying, "When the student is ready the teacher will appear."

Smiling at His incredible sense of humor, or maybe it was

His steadfast refusal to give up on me — I wasn't sure which; I closed the book, shut off the light, strapped on the headphones and pushed the button on the cassette player. Tired as I was, I preferred the Scriptures on tape.

"Faith comes from *hearing* the message and the message is *heard* from the word of God," I repeated to myself, reassured that I was doing the right thing.

I slept in a twin bed with thin white sheets. It reminded me of my childhood, sharing a room with my older brother, Don. Each TRC resident had to share a room with another "resident," who slept in his own flunky bed less than 10 feet away. My roommate snored like he still had an eight-ball of cocaine up his nose, and this went on every night, forcing me to learn patience *all* over again. My "anger' issue got no reprieve — it was tested repeatedly at night after being tested in the groups during the day.

"No rest for the angry," as the rageaholics on campus would say.

My Bible tapes were my only relief; and actually, it was my snoring, nose-monster of a roommate who ought to be thanking God for those tapes — and for me not whacking him in the head with my alarm clock in the middle of the night. I can almost hear all the "helpful" feedback now, as I imagine being forced to "process" the alarm clock incident in anger management group the next morning.

I shared the two-bedroom townhouse apartment with three TRC residents, all doctors: Jeff, a Southern "good ol' boy" pharmacist from Chattanooga, Tennessee, who ate more than his share of the highly addictive Oxycontin pills in his pharmacy; Sanjay, a histrionic anesthesiologist of Indian descent, whose drug of choice was the Fentanyl he was shooting up, and Mark, my roommate doctor from Austin, Texas, whose drugs of choice were porn and Klonopin.

The program was set up in such a way that it forced us to

break away from "self" and engage in a team-like attitude. We had to do everything in groups of threes. And that was about as much fun as having an ear ache and chewing tin foil. We were responsible for buying our own groceries, but we couldn't shop alone. Doing everything in groups of threes was another way of keeping people honest about their sobriety — through peer interaction and enforcement.

People snitched on each other all the time. If someone was caught off campus alone or with only one other person, their drug addict peers would rat 'em out in a heartbeat; and the violator would get punished. Punishment would normally mean the transgressor would have certain privileges removed; or worse yet, they would have to stay longer at TRC before being eligible to graduate — which meant they'd have to spend more money! Snitching on people cost them big money, which only made the violator hate the snitch even more.

Paying for church?

This rule about everything in three's even included church. Very few residents wanted to go to church on Sundays, so I ended up having to bribe a couple of guys to attend church service with me. And it was also a bit interesting that my paid "friends" and I were the only white guys in this awesome, all-black church, Community Fellowship Christian Church International.

The pastor, Jerome Dukes, was a mountain of a man. He stood over 6 feet 4 inches tall and had to weigh over 350 pounds, and his booming voice was as loud as he was huge. I "went forward" almost every Sunday that I was there, and he prayed over me like nobody before and nobody since! He knew the word of God and could preach it like few others I've ever heard, and his humor was gut-busting too.

Thank God for that church, as those sweet people loved on me every Sunday for over four months. Between Pastor

Dukes, the word of God, that sweet church family of faith and my New Testament tapes at night, I got what I needed. It was the medicine I needed to balance all the psychobabble I was hearing ad nauseum every hour all day, every day throughout my stay. Some of that psychobabble was useful too — but that balance was the key, as it is every time.

Chapter 8
"What's up Doc?"

Speaking of psychobabble, I remembered I had the obligatory meeting set with my assigned medical doc at TRC, a fellow by the name of Dr. Phil Wilson.

And only God knew what kind of psychobabble I was about to hear.

Maybe that's why He made sure I received Howard's letter at just the right time.

Howard Finkelstein, of the famed "Help Me Howard" segments on TV, encouraged me with his letter from back home. I will forever be grateful to Howard for truly being there for me, and for his very kind words:

> *"Take the time while in treatment, to look deep within you. You are in a place where you can learn tools for living while you've also been given a short respite from the day-to-day machinations of life. Use it to ponder questions that have haunted man since the beginning of time ...*

> *"What is God and what is my relationship with him? Who am I? What is the meaning of life?*

> *"Treatment facilities are like Club Med for the Head. Use the time and space to settle into yourself and find where the force that propels us all wants you to go....*

> *"In any case, I am here for you if you ever want to talk or just need someone to lean on. Be well. Be happy. Love others as others love you. We are all in this together.*

> *"Your friend, Howard Finkelstein."*

I needed to hear these things and begin to feel affirmed, as I was feeling down and almost out. God knew just when I needed to hear from Howard.

Just then, a gentle and unassuming man — who I assumed was Dr. Wilson — strolled into his office, interrupting my thoughts. He slowed his gait just long enough to give me a shy smile and shake my hand, while still navigating his way around my boots and his cluttered little desk.

He got right to business, even before his pants hit the seat. I was going to make small talk to schmooze with him a bit, but he had already put on his forensic hat and seemed bent on getting right down to figuring me out.

"Good luck, Doc," I thought to myself. "I've been trying for decades, and I'm still trying to figure me out."

Crossing his legs and placing the palm of his hand against his cheek — giving me his best Sigmund Freud look, Dr. Wilson quietly listened as I told him why I thought I was here.

"John, There are two types of depression: situational and clinical. You have both," he opined.

He had a gentle affect and was a quite likeable and affable gentleman in his early sixties. But that wasn't enough to make me surrender.

"You're a genius, Doc! I tell you I'm afraid of getting indicted — and that I've been drinking way too much vino to numb my fears, that I'm afraid of going to prison and missing my kids for a few years and messing their lives up too — and so you then conclude that I'm anxious and depressed — what did you call it, 'situational depression?' — and we both know I've gotta real *situation* here. *Now* I know why you get the big bucks! Doc, how long did you have to go to school to figure all that out?"

"John, your sarcasm is just another manifestation of rage or anger," Dr. Wilson calmly stated while leaning back in his swivel chair, his hands folded like one of those grandfatherly preachers. "You may need to be in our anger management group for just a little while."

"Where's Chief when I need him?" I asked myself aloud,

while thinking about that movie again, "One Flew Over the Cuckoo's Nest". The good doc asked, "Who's Chief?"

"Oh, nothing Doc, I'm just talking to myself, or maybe I shouldn't admit that? Let me ask you, Doc: If I admit I was just talking to myself, do you send me to the 'talking to yourself' support group too?"

He just leaned back further and stared at me, gracing me with a slight smile.

"You can send me to the talking to yourself group, the anger group, the sex addicts group, the wine drinking group, the cash is king group; send me to all the groups, Doc, cause let me tell you, I could use 'em all — better yet, send me to the federal camp and let's just get this whole stupid thing over with and I don't have to keep playing this game, whatdaya think?"

"Is that what you think this is, John, a game?"

"Doc, the only thing missing in here is your Sigmund Freud couch, where I lay down and tell you how I wasn't potty trained till I was in grade school or some such nonsense, and you periodically ask me, 'and how did that make you feel.'"

Dr. Wilson quit smiling, and he leaned forward and placed his folded hands on his desk. He was about to get serious on me, so I beat him to it.

"Dr. Wilson, why is it so hard to simply believe that I had manipulated and invented — through my own hand-picked forensic docs — my substance abuse problems — just to get in here and get outa dodge?"

He leaned back again.

"What's wrong with using my forensic doctor friends to help me when I'm jammed up like my clients? After all, they're the same guys I often pay to testify to the same good stuff on behalf of my clients. I knew what I needed them to say, and I knew what they needed to hear *before* they could say what I wanted them to say. It was *my* game plan, even if it wasn't in *their* playbook."

"Go on," is all he said.

"Dr. Wilson, it's not all that complicated, really; I needed help, and they could help me. The only rub: The 'help' I needed was legal defense help, I thought, but I couldn't just come out and say that."

He seemed to appreciate my honesty for a change, smiling a bit again.

"No decent doctor with any degree of integrity — and you can just imagine yourself, Dr. Wilson, or any of your colleagues — none of you would testify to what I needed, if I had just come out and said, 'Doc, I want to get out of a jam, so can you write a report saying, 'Contini's losing it; he's whacked, an addict with bipolar and paranoid tendencies,' the whole nine yards, so I can use your report and your testimony to get over on law enforcement, and get out of this jam?'"

He was smiling a bit bigger now.

Then I threw in some of the latest psychobabble I learned from the DSM-IV, the secular little bible embraced by all the shrinks, counselors, and recovery folks on the planet. All it did was get me into more trouble. Eventually, the staff actually put me on what they called "DSM-IV restriction," ordering me to stay away from their authoritative, coveted and diagnostic book of books.

"You and I both know, Dr. Wilson, that on certain levels, most shrinks want their patients to have the same exact issues or problems with which they themselves had once struggled. Perhaps then they might feel validated or less different, if everyone shared their issues and afflictions. Most of them are nut-jobs too, which is how they got into the field in the first place — often starting as a patient, right Doc?"

"You're going to be here awhile, John, you know that?" is all he said before finally busting a gut with laughter. He apparently couldn't hold it any longer. And the same with me — I laughed hard too. We both knew we liked each other. We had a good rapport, and we both knew that the truth lay somewhere in the middle — I wasn't as big a nut-case as I initially pretended, and yet I wasn't as healthy as I was still pretending.

Chapter 9

Talbott and the "Porterisms"

Tom Porter was a veteran counselor and a recovering addict. He was not as handsome as Rock Hudson, but not as rough looking as Joe Cocker either. Picture Marilyn Monroe getting together with Lurch from the Adams family. They get married and conceive a baby boy. He'd have grown up to look just like Tom Porter after a week of binge drinking. And yet, in spite of his history, Porter *still* had that magnetic twinkle in his eye whenever he'd smile big. His whole interesting face would suddenly spring to life like the six foot, five inch leprechaun that he was.

Porter drank so much in his life that he looked perpetually hung over, even decades into his sobriety. This made sense when you consider all his war stories, like the one he told us about how he rigged up his car so he could drink and drive with both hands still on the wheel! He had us howling one day in group when he shared how he drilled a hole in the firewall of his car so that the hose leading from his milk canister full of booze could travel from under the hood where it was strapped around the battery, into the driver's area, no problem.

He said a lot of other memorable things to us, and his own little proverbs are simply unforgettable.

"John, you are worried about what the folks back home are thinking about you? Hopefully you'll realize through your recovery this basic truth: 'What other people think of me is *none* of my business.'"

I had to stop and think about that, but then it stuck with me; and he was right; I had concerned myself *way* too much with what *others* thought about me and whatever I was doing, too concerned with how things would appear to others. I began to repeat that one to myself fairly often: "What other people think of me is none of my business."

Porter had a million of these helpful sayings, all keepers!

"It's not important for them to know; it's only important for me to know."

"Do the next right thing." (I must say that to myself a dozen times a day now.)

"I'm OK when it ain't OK."

"Trust God and clean house," he'd say fairly often.

"There are blessins' in lessons," was another of his favorites.

"If I'm not the problem, there is no solution."

Porter would often say, "I never speak more than when I listen."

My wife tells me that *that* particular proverbial "Porterism" is her favorite.

Porter kept it up all day long: "When I leave people alone, they leave me alone." He was driving home the point that we need to work on our *own* character defects, instead of taking the moral inventory of others.

All of us knew he was right, as even the fourth step of the 12-step program says to take "a searching and fearless moral inventory of *ourselves*." I found myself taking notes whenever this wise man spoke.

"Have an attitude of gratitude, be a pleasure to be around, and don't be negative. Listen, develop humility, get beyond pride, and quit trying to be the director. Be gentle with yourself."

Porter spoke obvious unadulterated truth, and coming from this "recovery-war" veteran of sorts, it carried that extra weight.

Just when I thought he was through, Porter would reload and blast us with still more sage advice: "Remove hate from your heart, live simply, give more and expect less."

I thought, "Give more and expect less. That's easy to remember, but harder to do."

Then he said, "Expectations are nothing but predetermined resentments."

"That's so true!" I said out loud to nobody in particular.

My affirming echo drew attention from other residents in the lecture, so I told myself to chill, and then I simply reflected on the truth and wisdom of what he had just said. If we visit our expectations on others, they will disappoint us almost every time. After all, they're only human, so by definition, they're imperfect. They'll almost invariably fail to meet our expectations and we'll end up resenting them! But why was this such a revelation to me, I wondered.

Tom Porter kept 'em coming: "When I say, 'develop humility,' what I mean is, 'don't think *less* of yourself, just think of yourself *less*.'"

I was so impressed with him that I scribbled down all these Porterisms, as I came to call them, on the back of business cards, or on whatever I could find, knowing I'd always want to keep them.

Then came Porter's buddy, Dr. Doug Talbott:

"If you ever want to know what it feels like to be someone you've never been before, try being yourself."

Ouch. "That can be so true," I told myself. "We're all trying to be someone we're not, and too often we're living a lie or trying to impress the next guy while not being ourselves."

Tag teaming us

Dr. Doug Talbott was the other elder "statesman," much like Porter, only he *owned* the treatment center. But unlike Porter, who looked as rough as he had lived, Talbott was a handsome man, sporting a nice head of white hair. He looked every bit like an older debonair trial lawyer, or better yet, an actor playing the part of an older debonair trial lawyer. He reminded me of the character Blake Carrington on the TV show *Dynasty*; or the Paul Newman character in *The Verdict*.

Both of these TRC giants stood as tall as me, well over 6 feet.

When Talbott spoke, it was like those old E.F. Hutton ads: everybody listened. One of Talbott's most memorable remarks was, "Living with me, wore me out."

We laughed out loud on that one, all of us in attendance that day.

Another great line from Talbott: "I've never met a person who has given me so much trouble as myself."

Again, more howling from the lecture audience.

These lines were memorable because we could *all* self relate, every one of us. Living with me, wore me out! I've never met a person who has given me so much trouble as myself! We knew that he was speaking unadulterated truth, because each of us in our own way had personified these sayings.

He advised, "If you're going through hell, keep going." When speaking of *real* sobriety, he'd remark, "There's a big difference between abstinence and sobriety. You can be abstinent and still not be sober; that just makes you a dry drunk — you still have no emotional sobriety."

Porter chimed in with: "Is lack of sobriety interfering with your life, or interfering with *who* and *what* you want to be? If you're allergic to something, stay away from it. You have to be comfortable in your own skin. You're not emotionally sober if you're restless, irritable, and discontent."

Every guy or gal in the room knew he was talking about him or her.

And then he said, "I don't have a drinking problem, I have a drinking solution. Look, if I, Tom, know that when I drink, I get in trouble, then why am I doing it? If you knew that every time *you* ate green beans, *you'd* get arrested, go to jail, lose your license, your family, your health and your money, you'd never eat another green bean."

I thought to myself, "Helloooo!"

They were tag-teaming us now, with the hand-off from Porter back to Talbott: "You can't *think* your way into sober *living*; you must *live* your way into sober *thinking*. If not now, when? If not *here*, *where*? You are not alone. Some of you are not ready, and if you haven't had enough pain, I can't teach you anything. When the student is ready, the teacher will appear."

My notes were almost illegible, I was writing so fast. The truth is something you *know* when you hear it, and I wasn't about to *not* write it down!

The doc continued with, "I was sick and tired of being sick and tired! You have to surrender to win. There are no victims, only volunteers."

Talbott said that often, almost as often as he said the Serenity Prayer:

"God grant me the serenity to accept the things I cannot change, the courage to change the things I can, and the wisdom to know the difference."

Speaking of the Serenity Prayer, I remember once copping an attitude about a staff member during my treatment on campus. I was apparently talking too much about my faith, when the "secular humanists" among the staff pounced on me, suggesting that I had an addiction to "religiosity." I remember arguing that if you have to be addicted to *something*, why not the word of God? They jumped all over me about being addicted to *anything*, in their arrogant "recovery speak."

That's when I snapped back, "Wait a minute. You 'healthy' folks are smoking like chimneys, hacking and coughing on every 15-minute break, and you're drinking coffee like you're Juan Valdez with your donkey double-parked on the corner. So don't tell me that everyone isn't addicted to *something*." I walked away angrily.

Tom Porter stopped me and said, "Let me ask you, John, which part of the serenity prayer is *not* working for *you* today?"

What a great line, a pointed question which cannot be

argued under *any* circumstances, no matter which way you try to cut it. The religion issue reared its ugly head again a little later. Both staff and residents were again harping on the "disease" of addiction — the big "D" as I called it. My very vocal opinion in the groups was that the "devil" was the big "D" behind the problem.

Tom Porter again stepped in as the quintessential peacemaker, the voice of reason. He said, "John, it doesn't matter which "D" is behind all this, whether it's the devil as you want to believe, or whether it's the "disease" of alcoholism by our definition; it's only important that you acknowledge the problem and get some help."

I grew to love these old guys over those four months.

The "rooms"

I picked up some of the best lines or sayings when I visited "the rooms" (i.e. the old guys in Atlanta refer to their AA meetings as "the rooms") in downtown Atlanta.

One of these sayings addressed the frustrating fact that addicts refuse to accept their condition even when multiple family members are urging them to get help. Their words too often fall on deaf ears. A visiting "addict" was questioning whether his family members were right in saying he was in denial, when one of the oldest black men chimed in: "Son, if three people call you a horse, you'd better saddle up."

"He nailed it," I thought to myself.

Another old black fellow in the rooms remarked one night, "Any time you become complacent, *come place* your ass in one of these seats." We all laughed at his style of delivery on that line, with his body language thrown in for extra measure and effect.

"If you always *do* what you always *did*, you'll always *get* what you always *got*." Then another old white guy piped up in a surprisingly animated fashion — in answer to a young guy's question (which doubled as wishful thinking) about the relative harmlessness of changing his drug of choice from cocaine to "simply drinking beer —"

"Boy," he replied, "changing your drug of choice is like changing seats on the Titanic."

By then, I was just shaking my head in amazement at the wisdom and logic of these old veterans.

Although I felt safe, I still didn't want to be here in Atlanta. I missed my family and felt embarrassed, fearful and ashamed; and yet on another level, I knew in my spirit that I was being blessed. I came to learn that the shame I felt was inappropriate. Shame was nothing but the sick sin of pride, the sin most despised by God.

The Old and New Testaments are replete with references to pride; for example, James 4:6 says: "God resists the proud and gives grace to the humble." Shame is only reserved for the individual who *needs* help and yet won't seek or accept it out of shameful pride.

I definitely learned this the hard and expensive way. It cost me $42,000 and four months of missing my family to learn this.

But, just when I thought I was good to go, I wasn't.

Chapter 10

Living in the Shadow of the Electric Chair

"Tell me, why do you think you drink more when you're in trial?" Dr. Talbott asked me.

"The pressure to be on, to perform, I guess," I replied, unsure of myself.

"Think about what you just said, John. It's the pressure to perform or be on, as you say, rather than the stakes to your client, that makes you want to drink more. I learned from the referring doctors, that you handled murder cases back in Ft. Lauderdale. I would have thought that the life or death of your client would be the *real* pressure, not the fact that you would have to perform well."

"Yes, of course, Dr. Talbott, but it really comes down to the same thing. If I'm not on top of my game and performing well, or if I drop the ball and I'm NOT on, then the guy's life could very well be forever impacted, and so naturally I feel a lot more pressure in trial."

"OK, John, fair enough. You feel more pressure in trial, and let's face it, there is indeed a tremendous amount of stress and pressure from what you describe; but is drinking alcohol the only thing we can do to address or alleviate that pressure? Is that your only coping mechanism? We've GOT to learn other coping mechanisms, John. And ask yourself, do you really feel ON the next morning or day in trial, after getting drunk the night before?"

"No, I hear you, Doc. I imagine I'm not as fast or sharp the next morning in court, especially if I'm hurting."

"Let me ask you this, John. Is the pressure greater when you think your client is innocent?"

"Exponentially greater, Dr. Talbott, which is why I hate the thought of representing the falsely accused. I know that sounds gutless, but who needs that kind of responsibility in their life? It's certainly a lot less pressure representing someone who did the deed, because then you can try as you might to get them help or minimize their plight. If there's a consequence and you did the *best* you could to help the guy, no harm, no foul, no sleepless nights; but if you have an innocent guy, doing your best may not be good enough."

"You don't have that fire in the belly or that passion to fight against the injustice of it all?" pressed the old doc.

"Not after the Willie Brown case, not anymore, at least not right now, Dr. Talbott."

"Tell me about this Willie Brown case. We've got some time."

Dr. Talbott then leaned back in his swivel chair and made himself comfortable for what we both knew would be an involved story. I followed his lead and sat back in a more relaxed fashion, even folding my legs like his. In fact, we both reached for the coffee cups that we had barely touched since the meeting began.

Then I just reenacted the whole crazy case for him, while his animated expressions and reactions encouraged me to get more specific:

...

"'I want a live line-up, and I want a polygraph, and I want it now!'

"Most folks in the crowded Fort Lauderdale courtroom had to be thinking, 'Can you believe this inmate, angrily screaming out like this from the jury box?'

"Willie Bernard Brown and another man, Roderick Christopher Mathis, were indicted on first-degree murder charges in the killing of Mark Noltion. The victim was fatally shot during an armed robbery, which took place outside the Melody Lounge in Pompano Beach on July 29, 1991. Mathis was the suspected triggerman and Brown was accused of being the accomplice in the slaying. I was in court that day because Judge Leroy Moe had appointed me to represent the very angry Brown.

"There were two rows of 'in-custody' defendants handcuffed in pairs and seated in the box of seats otherwise reserved for jurors. Showing respect for the inmates, I crouched down and finessed a squeeze play between the two rows of chairs, trying to minimize my size and presence and any disruption to the court.

"Just as I was bending down and whispering to Brown, 'I'm your lawyer,' he went into a maniacal rage and began beating the jury railing in front of him, yelling about the live lineup and polygraph."

"Boy, that must have shocked you," Talbott guessed.

"Oh yeah, to say the least. Everything in the courtroom stopped at once and I immediately said in his ear. 'Shut up, you idiot! You want this judge hating you?' That was not exactly the kind of warmth and compassion he might have expected from his own new lawyer. Maybe if I had imbibed a little more coffee, I'd have been better juiced up to handle the outburst."

"Speaking of coffee, you need a warm up?" graciously asked the good doc.

"Yes, please, and I want to thank you Dr. Talbott, for being so real and spending all this time with me."

"We're a family here, John, so don't think twice. It's all very interesting," he added, as he poured my refill. "Go on with the story."

"The bailiff scrambled over to get in Willie's face. The prosecutor, Brian Cavanagh, just looked at Willie with a priceless expression; and the people in the courtroom were looking half-horrified, but half-laughing too, because this was a real wild scene. It was arguably funny, like most things that break up the tension.

"All of a sudden, the stress in the courtroom was totally gone. The courtroom gallery was focused on this very volatile ongoing scene. Brown acted incredibly angry. He acted like he was innocent."

"What did the judge do when this happened?" Dr. Talbott asked, looking quite curious.

"A surprising reaction, actually, because as you might imagine, some judges would be just as vocal if an inmate-defendant raised his voice; but Judge Moe was quiet and reflective as he just leaned back and watched. Even though he was silent, he looked sharply at the other bailiff, essentially communicating: 'Get off of your old, New York-former cop-duff, and join your bailiff buddy over there and shut this guy up.'

"That's more his style, though he's always listening to every little thing that's going on. He doesn't miss a beat — he's a very introspective, analytical and deep person.

"Brown, who was cuffed and wore the inmate jumpsuit, was beyond just angry and demanding. He leaned way forward, visibly displaying his aggression. Nothing about him was passive; nothing apologetic or deferential — to the court or anybody else. He didn't care about anything except getting out of there. The image he projected was that of an innocent man accused of murder. It's an image I hadn't seen before, or since."

"I can believe it," Dr. Talbott offered, "and I imagine that's because you don't get too many innocent ones, is that right?"

"That's got to be a lot of it, but Willie also had a real strength or confidence about him. He was basically an angry or distrusting guy with a chip on his shoulder anyway — but given his circumstances, I can't say that I blame him. He didn't acquiesce to me very easily either.

"I told him 'I'm not doing a live line-up this early on. No depos have been taken, and there's been no discovery. You're gonna have to listen to advice from counsel. The tail's not wagging the dog here. I may be your lawyer, but it was the Judge who appointed me; and I'm going to do a good job. We need to take all the depositions, and I need to learn *everything* about your case, and then *maybe* I'll be in a position to do a live line-up and a polygraph.'

"Brown must have seen that I wasn't some milk toast, wimpy lawyer that he could intimidate. He was a small guy, but he was larger than life in his rage. Righteous indignation is what he projected, and he didn't care how he lashed out, or how it manifested itself. And I suppose that's how a lot of completely innocent people might react to being falsely accused of first degree murder."

"How did you get this case," Dr. Talbot asked, quizzically.

"When he was brought into court for his arraignment, he was unrepresented. Judge Moe questioned him about his finances and determined that Brown was indigent and therefore unable to afford private counsel. The judge then appointed me as his lawyer, at taxpayer's expense.

"The judge knew that I had experience with murder-one cases. I had recently won the high-profile murder case dubbed the "I-95" shooting case, and I'd already gone to trial on another major media case of triple murder, the Gil Fernandez case. And then there were the — no, I'm sorry, it wasn't until *later* that I went on to handle the murder-one cases for William Sawyer and Robert 'Fat Bobby' Yezdanian.

"Once I started getting into the case I learned that the courtroom scene wasn't the first time that Willie had flamed out in this case. Apparently, Pompano Beach Homicide Detective Greg Flynn was stunned a week earlier when Willie flew into a rage in *his* presence. Brown trashed the police photo line-up and other papers that Flynn had spread out on the visitor's table at the jail. I'm told that everything went flying."

"Really?" the doc reacted.

"This is what the detectives told the prosccutor. It was apparently reminiscent of that famous scene in the movie, *Five Easy Pieces,* when the Jack Nicholson character abruptly swept all the food, plates and glasses off the lunch table at a diner."

"I remember that famous scene," Talbott remarked, laughing.

"Well, imagine the waitress in that scene, and how she must've felt at that moment — probably just like Detective Flynn felt in the jail that day.

"Flynn's response, I'm told, was, 'I suppose this means you don't want to cooperate and help yourself?' To which Brown replied, 'Great deduction, Sherlock...did you learn that in the police academy?'"

"Oh, that's funny, but I'm sure it angered the detective," rightly guessed Talbott.

"It certainly did, so obviously, the jail visit by Detective Flynn didn't last long. Within moments, Flynn reported back to the veteran homicide prosecutor, Brian Cavanagh, who supposedly replied, 'If he wants to play that way, we'll accommodate him.'

"Eventually I deposed *everyone*. During those depositions, I discovered that the street witnesses did *not* identify Willie Brown the *first* time they were shown the photo lineup. And *that* was the red flag that also doubled as a seed of real doubt in my mind, that Brown may *not* have been involved in this murder."

"You mean they showed people the line ups more than once?" the smart old doc asked, with the right intonation of suspicion.

"It gets better, Dr. Talbott. And as you probably know, a photo line-up is a tool used fairly often by detectives when they target a certain suspect in their investigations. They will show the eyewitnesses a sampling of six photos that are typically glued or taped to a manila file folder. The involved photos are taken from books containing mug shots of assorted felons and other arrested individuals."

"Sure, John, I've watched enough TV like everyone else, to see how they do that."

"Well, Doctor Talbott, to make the line up *fair*, the depicted individuals need to look *somewhat* similar in appearance. The depicted individuals should not look markedly different, for example, with one guy appearing to weigh only 150 pounds while another guy is close to 250; and of course, they shouldn't have noticeably different skin pigmentation. Bottom line, the people in the photos are supposed to *somehow* fit the description of the target defendant."

"Of course," remarked Talbott, very involved in the story now.

"And because the detectives had suspected that Willie Brown was involved in this murder, they naturally included his picture as one of the six photos in the photo line up. But then throughout the depositions my conversation with each of the eyewitnesses was frighteningly similar:

"'You didn't identify *anyone* in the photo line up the *first* time the detectives showed it to you, did you?' I asked them. I was just guessing, but it worked out.

"'No,' they'd say.

"'It wasn't until they showed it to you again, a second time, that you identified Willie brown as being one of the guys involved in this homicide, isn't that right?' I continued.

"'That's right,' was the reply each time."

"Unbelievable," is all Dr. Talbott said, his face full of expression.

"Unbelievable, and yet true, and maybe *too* true, *too* often! I'm not so sure anymore. But in any event, the depositions went on for hours, eventually revealing the fact that the detectives had returned to the same street witnesses on a second occasion to present the same or a different line up, apparently unhappy with the results of the first interview.

"When initially interviewed by the detectives, the eyewitnesses failed to "ID" or identify Willie Brown as being involved in the homicide. They each testified in their respective depositions that they ID'd Willie Brown as the other guy in the homicide, *only* after being shown the line up a *second* time.

"Brown's photo, they said, was somehow *suggested* as one they might consider. This 'suggestion' was perhaps through a gesture or a detective's comment, 'You *sure* his picture is not among these?' This question was typically accompanied by a raised eyebrow and a certain intonation or inflection in the detective's voice, or worse yet, a gesture in the direction of Brown's photo! These are general indicators of what the appellate courts call a 'prejudicial, highly suggestive, impermissible' photo line-up."

"I would certainly think so," agreed Dr. Talbott.

"I eventually filed motions to dismiss the out of court ID's of Brown, based on all those inappropriate and suggestive things they had done. And of course, I attached the excerpts from these sworn, transcribed depositions; and it was then that I got the prosecutor's attention."

Chapter 11

Feeling the Heat

"You'd certainly have *my* attention, had I been the prosecutor in the Willie Brown case," Talbott acknowledged. "But what was your prosecutor like in this case? You see these guys on TV and you read about them in the papers, and I wonder if they get a bit hardened and jaded after years of hearing it all."

"That was my concern, Dr. Talbott, almost like 'the boy who cried wolf' story, where so many of these guys claim to be innocent, that when a *real* innocent guy actually comes along, nobody believes him — certainly no prosecutors believe him.

"But the prosecutor in Willie's case was Brian Cavanagh, a big, strapping Irishman. You'd love the guy. He's this ruggedly handsome guy with a handlebar mustache, a real penchant for theatre, and a love for the English language. He is a modern day Shakespearean orator, and passionate to the bone."

"Sounds like a real character," Talbott remarked, laughing a bit.

"Oh for sure, and if Brian believed you were guilty, you knew it, and so did everyone else in the courtroom, and those down the hall too! It's always a dramatic scene when Cavanagh works himself up in front of the jury — his voice booms and his face turns all red. The jurors typically become visibly nervous and worked up too, as they become part of this real life courtroom drama."

"Wow, I'd love to see this guy in action," the doc stated, smiling ear to ear.

"You really would, Dr. Talbott, because Cavanagh would typically co-opt these jurors into *his own* Broadway play of sorts! It's true, they unwittingly become actors in his own theatrical Shakespearean tragedy. Everything works out great for Brian Cavanagh and for the homicide victim's family, as long as the jurors stick to the script and find the defendant guilty, of course."

"I see," replied Talbott as he stroked his chin, with a look that told you he could actually visualize Brian Cavanagh doing his thing with the jury.

"But the whole event becomes a much more complex and real life tragedy for Cavanagh if the jurors don't follow the script. And this is *exactly* what happened in the Fat Bobby murder trial when Cavanagh and I battled it out in another murder trial. My guy, Fat Bobby, walked on that case, and you would have loved to have watched all the theatre in that case."

"Oh, I'd love to hear about *that* one some time too," Talbott offered.

"Remind me to tell you about it, Dr. Talbott. The fat Bobby murder trial with Cavanagh is something for the record books, really. Unforgettable, to say the least.

"But in this one with Willie, perhaps it was a little harder for Cavanagh to play that dramatic role of righteous indignation, because Willie Brown was already playing it! Cavanagh wasn't accustomed to this kind of behavior coming from the *defendant.*

"It got so bad that I didn't want to risk going to trial, as lame and gutless as that sounds — because I eventually came to believe that my client Willie was innocent! And I really hear myself sounding gutless when I say this, but it's true, I always felt that representing the innocent was just way *too* much pressure."

"Really," asked Talbott, with surprise in his voice and facial expression.

"Absolutely, because for me — representing the guilty is a *lot* less pressure. Think about it, Doc, it's hard to lose a lot of sleep when one of the *rightfully* accused gets convicted. But what if the innocent guy gets convicted? I can't imagine the sleep deprivation I'd suffer then."

"You realize what you're saying, John? You're thinking about *you*, and how *you* feel, not *them* or how *they* feel. Do you really *hear* yourself?"

"Yes, and I make no bones about it Doc. It is all about me and protecting my feelings, I admit that."

"No wonder you drink, John. If you get outside yourself and focus instead on others — even these guilty people and how they feel — then you'll be OK, but not until then."

"But when representing innocent people, the unbelievable pressure I feel..."

"There you go again, John, what *you* feel — what about what *they* feel? That's your calling as a lawyer. You've chosen to be the one who has to step up to the plate and help others, regardless of guilt or innocence."

"I know I chose that, but that doesn't mean I have to love or embrace the overwhelming pressure that comes with defending the *innocent* guy. I'd much rather defend the guilty, it's true, because I *do* feel less pressure, and *they* know what they did and they're grateful for the help."

Talbott just sat back and listened, with a look of compassion on that old handsome face.

"I get a chance to encourage them and share my faith, without feeling like I'm standing in the middle of a crowded I-95 with trucks coming at me doing 90 mph. And while I'm being so honest, I'd have to say I always feel like drinking more of that fine red wine when I represent the innocent.

"And while we're talking about it ... Can you imagine an actually innocent, falsely accused guy in *real* life, leaving his fate in the hands of a motley jury of strangers — retired school teachers and plumbers and neighbors, people focused on getting out of there in time to pick up their kids or watch Andy Griffith — especially in a murder case, when the individual is facing the ultimate penalty?"

"You hearing yourself, John? So much for having faith in the system, huh? You're in the right place to take a break, my young friend, and re-think *all* of this — and whether you're still up for all this heavy murder stuff, the trials, the pressure."

"Doc, I already love you, I really do, but you and I might as well quit jerking one another around with all this alcoholism stuff. I'll *never* be totally convinced I'm an alcoholic — and in fact, I'm telling you now that I'd bet you big money I'm *not*, though I might in fact be an addict. Oh, by the way, the fact that I just said I'd bet you big money, does that mean I've got an addiction to gambling too?"

"Now John — "

"Wait just a second, please Doc, let me just get this off my heart, so I don't feel like I'm being a fraud with you. I respect you way too much to not be brutally honest with you.

"I have an addictive nature and personality, for sure, and I have no problem admitting to that; but does that mean I ought to label myself an alcoholic, and that I can no longer defend murder clients, because I enjoy the buzz and relaxed feelings I get from a glass or two of red wine?"

"John, John — "

"Almost done, Doc, and while I'm getting real with you, let me tell you respectfully, Dr. Talbott, that this whole nomenclature, label or word, 'alcoholic,' is so ridiculously wrong and even misleading to what *you* guys are saying *yourselves*, that you really ought to initiate a change in the recovery community to correct it. You'd have a lot more people like me jumping in the pool if you didn't assign the wrong disease label and inflammatory word to the problem with our *thinking*.

"You say it has nothing *really* to do with alcohol, per se, and you even have the saying, 'the 12 step program doesn't treat your *drinking*, it treats your *stinking thinking*,' and yet you call yourselves and everyone else with *stinking thinking*, 'alcoholics,' focusing in on the drinking again."

"You done, John?" Dr. Talbott quietly and politely asked, smiling a bit too big for my enjoyment, while leaning back and stretching like he knew we'd be there a while longer than expected.

"Just about, Dr. Talbott. I'm just saying, I have no problem admitting I have an addictive nature, and you yourself even told us they're gonna call all these addictions 'OCD' within the next 10 years — that the *thoughts* are the *obsessions* and the *acts* are the *compulsions,* hence the reason they'll call it all 'Obsessive Compulsive Disorder,' so I'll even admit to having some of this OCD thing going on.

"If there are two pizzas sitting here, Dr. Talbott, I'll eat 'em both if you don't join me; if there's a pot of coffee, I'll drink the whole pot whether you have a cup or not. I have that addict mentality, 'if one's good, two's better.' And we both know that this isn't always true at all.

"Oh, I've got the character defects that the 12-step program speaks of. And I need to surrender to my Higher Power every few *minutes* — not just every day like the program suggests in the very first step, I'll grant you that all day long."

"Let me know when you're through, John," he said, this time sitting up and not smiling.

"I'm done, but I can't imagine what you're gonna say that'll convince me that this has *anything* to do with being called an 'alcoholic;' or why my addictive, OCD-type nature, when it comes to food or coffee or sex or money, ought to earn me *your* label of 'alcoholic.'

"Sure, now I'm done, so tell me now why if I drink that whole pot of coffee, I ought to call myself an alcoholic, with the obvious word *'alcohol' right there* within the root word *'alcoholic,'* despite the fact that we're talking about coffee, for heaven's sake!"

"Take a breath, John, as I tell you *why* I think you *are* just like the rest of us. The fact that the word or label upsets you so much is half my case. If you knew in your heart that you were not, you wouldn't let it bother you at all and you probably wouldn't even be here.

"John, what you *really* need to do is have an honest conversation with *yourself*, perhaps, and not so much with me, though I do enjoy talking about these things with you. If you were to truly *hear* yourself, John, you are almost coming at me as an interrogation of sorts; but what you *really* want to do, in my opinion, is have an interrogation with the soul — *your* soul, as I have had to do in my life.

"And it's hard to do that when you're feeling the heat. As I told you before, you didn't see the light and *then* decide to come here — like just a few have done before you. *You* came here like *most* of the folks who were facing real difficulties, feeling the heat. And until you surrender to win and see the light— until you have that sort of interrogation of your own soul — you will no doubt be defensive about these labels as you call them."

Chapter 12

The Road to Surrender

He could see right through me. That is why Dr. Talbott was the top dog. Everyone looked up to the old man, and I was one of his biggest fans.

My respect for the man was immediate, as I remember asking myself, "How could you be a street bum earlier in life and then turn it around and look this good, and now be a classy, nationally renowned doc and own your own recovery joint?"

Our lecture sessions with Dr. Talbott only caused our level of respect for him to exponentially increase. He was real, and he was funny. His war stories made you want to cry as you were laughing so hard. But then you'd almost hurt for his victims, until you learned that he had reconciled with his family and had "cleaned up all the carnage from the wreckage in his past," as he explained.

To top it off, he *still* looked like a million dollars, and we were all paying good money to be in *his* acclaimed facility. It was this kind of unparalleled respect for the man — or perhaps it was just my conscience that day — that compelled me to tell him the "truth," that I *really* didn't need to be there, that I really wasn't like these other addicts.

"Dr. Talbott," I began, "I gotta be real with you. You're *big* on telling the truth; well, the truth is, I convinced the forensic docs back home to send me to treatment, and I only came here to hide from the feds back home. They were targeting me for reasons that might not matter, and all that mattered to me was building a mental health defense in case I was indicted. My purpose in coming here wasn't honest at all — I just needed to get outa dodge, hide for a while and build that defense."

Dr. Talbott's response was as quick as his smile: "John, as I told you yesterday, addicts don't see the light, they feel the heat."

"But Dr. Talbott —"

He smiled even bigger and put his hand up like a kind traffic cop, letting me know it was his office and his turn to talk.

"Most people are here for treatment to escape trouble back home, John; often it's trouble with a spouse or family members who do an intervention and threaten to leave them if they don't come here. Some people are here because they're in danger of losing their careers. Many of your doctor friends here seeking treatment are dealing with license problems. In just as many cases, people like you come here because they're in danger of getting arrested and losing their liberty."

He could see that I was trying to sit up and speak again so he motioned ever so gingerly for me to sit back and listen. I did.

"You may have *thought* you were being deceptive and fooling folks in coming here, but were you? God can use your own deception, John, to get you the help that *He* knows you really need."

"He's right," I thought. "I really don't know what the truth is anymore." But old habits die hard, as I kept pleading my case, not wanting to surrender.

"Dr. Talbott, but what if I *really* fooled the docs back home, and then *they* poisoned the well with you guys here in Atlanta, so you and your staff end up believing the very docs I conned back home? And just for good measure in keeping up the con, I threw in some good stuff when I first got here. So why is it so hard for my wife and you guys to believe that I was just *working* everyone, to get out of a jam?"

Then he got me: "John, your best thinking got you here."

Then tapping his forehead with his index finger, he said, "You're fighting behind enemy lines — you're thinking too much. You remind me of *me* when I was younger. Get out of your head. It's dangerous up there. We'll never know the real truth, John, and that *is* your fault, if you *insist* on finding fault somewhere. But fault's not important now; it's only important that you be honest *now*, with *yourself*. What's the truth *now*?"

My response was quick: "The truth? I really don't know anymore. I'm at the point now where I no longer know where my deception ends and where the *real* truth begins."

Dr. Talbott replied, "That's the problem with being dishonest over time with everyone, it becomes pathological — you do it so often that you don't know when you're doing it, and then you don't even know when you're being dishonest with yourself. It's called denial."

It was virtually impossible to argue against this logic and the unadulterated truth of what he was saying.

He continued, "It's not just the drinking and the drugs that get people into treatment, John. It's the circumstances they virtually create for themselves. You're here because you had a problem. The drinking is only symptomatic of the underlying root cause of the problem, and you are simply self-medicating as an ineffective attempt to numb the pain and avoid dealing with the issues. You're in the right place, John, and you might as well process this stuff *now*. Life won't get any easier until you do."

"How can I argue with this man, a veteran doctor I respect so much," I thought to myself.

"Recovery is not for people who *need* it, John, because *everyone* needs it; it's for people who *want* it. You've got to *want* to get well and get healthy, mind, body and spirit. Everyone *needs* to process their issues John, and those who say they don't, well, they're the ones who need help the most."

I finally said, "OK," choosing then and there to surrender to win.

From that moment on, I just started unloading on him. I talked and talked — and then I talked some more and eventually dumped my whole bucket, releasing all the guilt and shame that I'd been harboring; and before I knew it, I started feeling better. It was actually quite cathartic.

It was only then, after my conversation with Dr. Talbott, that my "treatment" truly became voluntary. Helping others even became a motivation for me, as I wanted to stay and finish what I started and graduate. Even that elusive gold coin you get after graduating from TRC was attractive.

Added to the mix was the fact that I simply had to guard against leaving "against medical advice" or "AMA" as they call it. There it remained, my own pathology; it was rearing its preemptive legal head yet again. The whole "AMA" thing could hurt me later, I figured, as I was *still* in survival mode, protecting myself and playing defense lawyer, just in case the feds were sandbagging me.

Somewhere along the way I'd forgotten the old saying, "a lawyer who defends himself has a fool for a client."

"Better finish, it'll look better," I thought to myself, "just in case."

My wife still occasionally calls me "J.I.C." because I'm always preemptively approaching life's decisions with this unbending mentality, often saying "just in case."

Sticking around helped me to understand my "family of origin" issues, as they are called, forced to appreciate the truth of all my character defects. It was hard to argue with the staff over their diagnosis of my "low frustration tolerance" and my "anger issue," especially when I reflected on the time I had threatened another resident.

Masqueraded fear

Nofal was an Arabic guy who ratted me out for leaving TRC with just one other resident and not two as the rules required. The rules also require residents to snitch on each other for *any* rule violation, ostensibly to guard against the violator's relapse. The thought process is, if people start sneaking off and violating the simple rules, it wouldn't be long before they violated the more serious rules and began using alcohol and drugs again.

I was supposed to have gone to church on that Sunday in a group of three, then back to campus. Two of us dropped off the third after church and then we went out to the Lenox Mall in Buckhead, the upscale section of Atlanta.

It got back to me that Nofal intended to tell the staff in "process group" the next day of my transgression, so being the sweet-spirited guy I was, I angrily threatened to do some bodily harm to him. It was an otherwise empty threat, but I wanted him to think twice about ratting me out. My threats only gave him more things to "process" that next day, compounding my problems.

Tomorrow came and Nofal and I were in the group with a half dozen other people and two staff therapists, Nanci Stockwell and Tina Thompson. Nofal started to mimic me and my threats from the night before so I got uglier with him. I called him a camel jockey and asked him to imagine my size 14 boot in his otherwise homely face; and when he started to bark back at me, I remember abruptly moving to the edge of my seat in a most menacing fashion, gritting my teeth and telling him that I'd rip out his larynx and puke down his throat. Suffice it to say it was a nasty visual, designed to horrify.

In complete unison and without uttering a syllable, Nanci and Tina directed me out of the room. Nanci simply reached over from her chair and opened wide the door, while each therapist motioned with the back of her hand for me to exit.

As I walked toward the door eyeballing Nofal, Nanci said, "I will meet you in my office."

I sat alone in her office for the remaining 10 minutes of the group, before she joined me. She pulled her chair closer to mine and sat across from me.

"Why did you do that, John?" she quietly asked, leaning forward in her chair and fixing her sensitive gaze on me.

I just sat there, speechless, wondering why.

"Why did you react so strongly?" she added. "What were you afraid of?"

She was not threatening at all. Her approach and genuine concern for me made me more concerned about myself, so I questioned my level of anger, which I then learned was really *fear*.

"Anger is simply masqueraded fear, John," she opined.

Whether that should or should not have been a revelation to me, it *was*. I remember repeating this to myself, "anger is nothing but masqueraded fear."

Nanci showed me how this relatively *minor* transgression the day before was then exponentially compounded by me into a *major* problem — all because of my fears precipitating my reaction to Nofal's disclosure. I had a total lack of emotional sobriety.

I knew one thing for sure. I had more work to do on myself.

She was dead on right, telling me that my anger was only 'masqueraded fear.' This forced me to confront my fears, to try to understand their origins — and then it made sense that I was *fearful* because I knew I'd be kept at TRC *longer* as a result of Nofal's disclosure of the violation; and this fear was quickly exacerbated because my mind took my longer stay and did the math, forcing the logical deduction that I'd therefore have to pay TRC *more* money — their daily rate for continued stay until ready for discharge.

The extra money was real money that I worried about *not* having; and the extra time at TRC also meant more time *away* from my family, and I already missed my family tremendously. These fears were the source of the anger and the outburst, though not an excuse.

What especially amazed me was the fact that I could react in this un-Christ-like way toward Nofal within 24 hours of having that spirit-filled church service the day before, and even after listening to the Bible tapes the night before the outburst.

"God's got a lot more work to do on me," I recall thinking.

My humor was often inappropriate too, according to staff. One of the TRC shrinks diagnosed me as possibly being "bipolar" upon learning of my violent remarks toward Nofal, so I was asked to "process" this diagnosis in group the next day. That was a mistake.

"I think you *are* bipolar," Susan said, turning to laugh and seek approval from the group. Nanci tried to admonish her for not self-relating, but I beat her to the punch.

"I'd rather be bipolar than bisexual, sweet lips," I responded, resulting in yet another reprimand for being insensitive and politically incorrect toward others in the group, who may not have shared my sexual orientation. But even mean-spirited Susan couldn't help but laugh.

The doctors, Nanci my therapist, and the rest of the TRC staff nonetheless *eventually* decided that I was ready to be a "mirror-image counselor" and help with new residents. The name refers to the fact that the mirror image counselor could figuratively see *themselves* when they were *first* admitted to TRC, as the "image" in the "mirror" of sorts, when hearing the excuses and the rationalizing of the newly admitted residents.

Before I could help the new residents face the truth about themselves, I had to first mirror what it meant to face the truth about myself. It became obvious that I had used my excuses and rationalizing to keep my Heavenly Father out of my struggle. On some level, I wanted God to help me; but on another level, I wanted to have that "God in a box to go," or to keep God on the periphery of my life so *I* could be the one *in control* of my life. But the truth is, I was out-of-control. Seeking the freedom to say and do whatever I impulsively wanted to do, I had essentially imprisoned myself in chains and bondage of fear and anger.

Reflections

Remembering that Christ said *He* was "the *truth*," I now have more appreciation for what He also promised in John 8:32, "...and the *truth* shall make you free." There it is again, the fact that only *He* — the "truth" — can make me "free" from these obsessions and addictions. I had wasted a lot of time struggling alone and trying to beat these things in my own power, before I finally surrendered to win.

Addiction, I've learned, is rooted in self-centeredness. I've come to learn that just like most folks, I'm basically addicted to "more," more of *everything* — more food, more money, more sex or love, more admiration, more fame, more respect, more of whatever there is to get.

Dr. Talbott stressed that we, as humans, have an insatiable appetite for sex, for instance; the more you get, the more you want and need. The libido is not satisfied by sex, it is stimulated by sex; so the more you get, the more you want or think you need from others. It becomes a giant self-defeating process, not unlike a crack addict thinking that more crack will satisfy the need.

Instead of being addicted to "more," I've had to learn that "less is more," as my wife often says. We need to become content and satisfied with what we *already* have and who we *are*, just as the Apostle Paul told us over 2,000 years ago.

As recorded in Philippians 4:12, Paul wrote, "I know what it is to be in need, and I know what it is to have plenty. I have learned the secret of being content in any and every situation, whether well fed or hungry, whether living in plenty or in want."

The the secret of being content is actually in Paul's next comment, as recorded in Philippians 4:13, "I can do all things through Christ who strengthens me." That's it — through *Christ*, with *His* help, I can beat *all* of these things.

Sean Mulcahy, a diminutive priest in Hallandale Florida

with a strong Irish brogue, once told me, "True spirituality, John, is *not* about adding *more* spiritual things to your world. It's not about addition; it's about subtraction."

One thing is for certain. There is no beating our issues alone; we need the help of our Higher Power, and we absolutely need to "surrender to win." That's why they call the Gospel the "Good News." It doesn't matter who you are or what you've done — He is there for you! You don't get cleaned up *before* you come to Him; He cleans you up *after* you come to Him, just as you *are*. There is nothing you can do to make Him love you *more*, and there's nothing you can do to make Him love you *less*.

He is all about having our obsessions and compulsions lifted from us. The same is true of the good news of the gospel. Addicts aren't the only ones who feel the heat before seeing the light; countless men and women turn to God and are brought into the family of faith through addiction, adversity, tragedy, fear, loss, loneliness, arrest, prosecution, jail and prison, or any number of other painful or frightening scenarios.

I pray that my children will not need to actually experience these painful or frightening scenarios before accepting these truths that too many of us stubbornly learned the hard way. Hopefully, my kids will take the easier road, simply embracing the wisdom of the Bible's proverbs. I pray that they will heed the sage advice of informed people like Tom Porter and Doug Talbott, and the wisdom of all the old men in "the rooms," advice that comes from real experience.

Chapter 13

Calling Home

"I love you Kaaathleen ... Oh yes I doooo ...I don't love anyoooone ... quite like youuooo ... When you're not withhhh me ... I'm blueoooooo ... Oh Kaaathleen, I love youuooo.

"Can I sing one more song to you, Baby, before we say good night?"

"OK, Daddy," my precious Kathleen whispered into the phone, almost asleep.

"Edelweiiiiss, edelweiiis, every morning you greeeeet me ... Soft and whiiiite, clean and briiiight, you look happy to meeeet me ... Blossoms of snow, may you bloooom and grooow, bloooom and grooow, foreeeever ... Edelweiiiss, edelweiiiss, bless my Kathleeen foreeever.

"I love you, Kathleenchan."

The silence on the other end of the receiver told me that my little 10-year-old angel was fast asleep.

"Good night, Sweetheart, sweet dreams," I told her spirit and subconscious.

I didn't expect a response, and yet I felt a real longing to hug her close to me and kiss her head as I always did. Sadly, I'd have to wait till this whole Atlanta thing was behind me — and that was the hardest thing I've ever had to do.

I was tempted many times to run home and get my fix of the family, but that meant leaving TRC "AMA" or against medical advice, which would have decimated my entire mental health defense in the event of still uncertain prosecution. To run with my feelings would've been impulsive and selfish, I knew, so the big picture dictated that I suck it up and stay the course.

...

The next night I spoke first with my wife Elizabeth. I was

overwhelmed with how much emotion was building up, but I kept it simple.

"Elizabeth, I want you to know that I appreciate all you're doing back there with the kids and keeping it all together."

"I know you do, Honey, but try not to worry. The kids are so busy with dance, gymnastics and basketball, and then with their church friends, and getting ready for traveling to see your Dad in Ohio, and then again to see my relatives in Texas; they have no time to wonder what's wrong or to worry."

"Am I really that irrelevant? The way you make it sound, they haven't missed a beat."

"Of course they miss you. They love their Daddy and can't wait to see you. But I thought you'd want to know that everyone's doing great. And that really should help you relax and feel good."

"It does, and I don't mean to sound so needy, but this whole thing's taking too long — and as insecure as this sounds, I don't want them to get used to not having me around. And yet I don't want them crying and sitting around worrying about their daddy either, because that would only make this worse. I just can't wait till I get to be with everyone again. I'm sorry about everything, Baby."

"It's OK, John — it's all going to work out, and we'll all be better for it as a family."

"Thanks, Sweetheart, for everything. Things will be better when this is all over. I'll make it up to you. I love you," I replied.

"By the way John, Pastor Larry Thompson called. It was the sweetest thing. He is so sweet, Honey. You know what he said?"

"No, what?"

"He asked me if we needed any money to help with the bills while you're gone. Wasn't that incredibly thoughtful of him?"

"That only makes me feel worse," I replied, letting my sinful pride get in the way.

"Well don't," she countered, "that's not from God. It should just remind you of how blessed we are to have a church family, and that your pastor loves us. I let him know we were OK, but just the fact that he *asked* is so sweet. I love our church, John. I thought you'd be thrilled to hear that he was thinking of you — and of *all* of us."

"I know, and for *you* guys, I am. It's me, Elizabeth. I feel embarrassed is all, that Larry would feel the need to have to step in and be the provider for my family. He's awesome, don't get me wrong."

"John, he's not trying to be the provider. He knows — just like we *all* know — that *God* is the real provider for our family. He uses *you* most of the time, Honey, but it's still God who provides for all of us, right?"

"I know, I know," I deferred, "but do you know how many people in the church would want to puke into the offering plate, if they knew a portion of their money in that plate went to some lawyer's family, because he ran off to rehab to get outa dodge?"

"John, I got the impression he was offering his own personal help — from himself and Cynthia — not from church offerings. He obviously cares, and I wanted you to know just how much we're loved, and how much he loves you too."

"Wow," is all I could mutter, as I made a mental note to write a letter of appreciation to Pastor Larry. I then remembered how concerned he looked when I tearfully confided in him that fateful day at the church. "I do love Larry, Sweetheart, and I'll tell him in a letter soon, OK?"

She said some other sweet and encouraging things to me before saying goodnight, and then I asked to speak *first* to our nine-year old boy, Johnny.

"You daddy's boy, Johnnychan?"

"Yes, I'm daddy's boy!"

"You make me smile, Johnny. I'm the proudest daddy in the whole wide world, you know that?"

"Thank you."

"Who's daddy's personal hero?"

"Me!"

"That's right, Johnny, and don't ever forget that, OK?"

"OK."

"I love you soooo much, Johnny. And I miss you, Buddy, more than you could ever know. I can't wait to see you next weekend."

"Me too. When is your job done there?" Johnny innocently asked, oblivious to his daddy's hidden agenda and machinations.

"I'm still working to finish things here, Johnny," I replied, struggling to find the right words or version of doublespeak that wouldn't be a *literal* lie.

"I *was* working to finish things here," I told myself, justifying my lie by omission. Uncomfortable with this moment of dishonesty with my own son, I switched the subject to the only One who could help me.

"Can I say a prayer before bed, Johnny?"

"OK," he replied.

It's hard to describe the ache in my heart or the emptiness I was feeling as I began to pray with my son. I was trying not to cry. I didn't want to cry on the phone. It was all I could do to try to talk while fighting back the emotion, but then as I prayed, the heaviness suddenly lifted and the peace of God came over me.

"Thank you, Father, for this precious, precious boy, Daddy's personal hero. Please protect him from any harm, Father, and surround him with your angels tonight. Same with Kathleen and Mary and Mommy, and everyone else in the family we love so much, Father. He is such a good boy, Lord, and he loves you so much. Please reunite us as soon as possible, Lord, so we can be together again every day and every night, forever and ever. By the power of the Holy Spirit, and in Jesus' name, Father, we ask *all* these things. Amen."

It must've been a Sprit-thing how everything felt all right again when the prayer was over. I knew at that moment that only God could do that.

"Good night, Daddy. I love you."

"I love you too, Johnny, more than life itself. Before I hang up, may I speak with Mary and Kathleen now, Johnny?"

Johnny shouted for his sisters as I emptied the pool of tears that had suddenly welled up in my eyes.

"Daddy!" shouted my little Mary into the phone, then only four years old.

"Marychan! I love you sweetheart."

"Come home, Daddy. When are you coming home?"

Ouch again.

"Soon, Marychan — as soon as I can, OK?"

She wanted a more definite response, so I struggled to give her the same answers I'd given Johnny about finishing the work I had started. And then, thank God, she let me pray for all of us and sing to her before passing the phone to her sister. Still more prayers and *more* songs for Kathleen, and only then could I sleep in peace.

Chapter 14

Triple Venti Mocha

"Our sickness lies in our secrets," Thurmon told me.

That remark had a huge impact on me, because I immediately recognized it as truth. Thurmon Strother was one smart dude, and what an incredible testimony he had. This former longhaired doper and drug dealer had survived both the bad guys and the good guys, escaping near death and prison too. He had truly gone straight, gotten educated, had now come full circle and was thankfully helping the rest of us.

Thurmon was a tall and impressive, good looking man, sporting a chiseled beard, short hair, fine threads and very gentle affect that belied his appearance and past. And he was one of the most *loved* counselors at TRC, personifying the kind of warm demeanor you'd imagine Christ as having.

"Stick around, John," Thurmon told me, "don't leave before the miracle."

"Nanci Stockwell tells me that every week. But Thurmon, I think you got that really awesome saying, 'our sickness lies in our secrets,' from the source of all *real* knowledge, the Bible."

"There you go again, John." He was shaking his head and smiling. Thurmon was letting me know that he thought I was still struggling with what he once called my addiction to religiosity.

"No, seriously Thurmon, I'm not taking away from your cool recovery slogans — these truths that can *absolutely* benefit us; but I'd like to think you'd *want* to know that you're actually being *affirmed* by what James — Jesus Christ's half brother — said over 2,000 years ago."

"OK, you got me, what did old James have to say?"

"'Confess your faults one to another, and pray one for

another, that you may be healed.' It's recorded in James 5:16, in case you're even *remotely* interested. I just knew that you'd want to see that the apostles — famous guys like James — absolutely agree with you."

We were both smiling. He knew I was already a fan of his.

"It's nice to be on God's side," Thurmon replied. "Now don't ever forget, John, there's *healing* in *feeling*."

"All kidding aside, Thurmon, thank you for *everything*. I *really* appreciate you." We did the bear hug thing for our good byes, as I silently repeated his words, "There's healing in feeling."

…

Before you could say, "grown men regressing as frat boys," six of us piled into Tommy's white suburban.

"Hey Tommy," Sanjay joked while claiming the front seat, "why does a urologist like you have a big long suburban, unless that's a phallic thing?"

The rest of us began laughing, but nobody harder than Sanjay who loved to laugh at his own jokes. None of us could imagine Sanjay as the addicted anesthesiologist high on whatever he was shooting, because he was so wild even as we knew him straight.

We pulled into our usual spot at Barnes & Noble like a carload of freshman crashing a sorority party. The three other nut jobs followed Sanjay to the music section in the back of the bookstore as Tommy and I went for our drug of choice, caffeine.

"May I have a triple venti mocha, dry, with a shot of sugar free vanilla?" Tommy asked, like he'd done it a million times before.

"That sounds like Starbucks, so I am not so sure I know what you would like in your coffee, Sir."

She was probably twenty, if that, and adorable. She had long shiny brown hair and perfect ivory skin and big brown eyes, too cute to not look at for another couple minutes, and Tommy did like the young women. It had gotten him in trouble in his marriage before — more than once, only this time his wife told him he'd better get it right or it's the last time. He blamed his sexual addiction problem on the pills, which is why he was working the whole TRC gig. It was apparently easier to sell it to his wife that way, since she, like most of the wives, preferred to think that his problems were found in these terrible little pills rather than the core of his being.

"But it says Starbucks, sweetheart, right there behind your pretty little face — on the Starbucks sign," Tommy teased, smiling big and flirting with her.

"That means we sell Starbucks coffee, Sir, but we're *still* Barnes & Noble." She was smiling too and turning red, which only encouraged a guy like Tommy, who was old enough to be her father.

"We have espresso drinks and we can give you three shots, if you want, but I'm not sure what you mean by 'dry' or 'venti.'"

I started off patiently watching this charade mostly for Tommy's benefit, though I was jonesing for my caffeine fix. He almost needed an audience to play to, I knew, because I was very much like him. Tommy and I had become best friends at TRC, cut from the same cloth. We were each a Johnny Carson type and we needed an Ed McMahon to pull off the best part of our act. It was the sport of it all that almost compelled him to flirt like this. Old habits die hard, and I knew this better than anyone. I lived it for years. You perform better and really get on top of your game when your buddies are watching.

"While you two get close to each other, can I have a regular cup of coffee, no fancy nothing, just plain black coffee, no frills," I interrupted, unable to fake patience anymore.

"Now, now, my recovering friend, you're going to frighten

the young lass. Where is all this hostility coming from? You may have to process that in group tomorrow," Tommy joked, oblivious to the level of my caffeine addiction.

He leaned back toward her and poured on some more charm as she smiled bigger and poured my boring cup of coffee, just to get rid of me. Their syrupy exchanges were enough sweetener for me, so I opted for the bitter black coffee as a reminder of my own circumstances. Then, I thought, maybe I was in a foul mood because I just found out that I'd be missing out on a family trip with Elizabeth and the kids. They were going to Texas without me to visit with her relatives.

"Snap out of it, John," I told myself, "and enjoy your new buddies at TRC and all the time and space you always longed for!"

Then I remembered the truth of what my father used to tell me. "People always want what they haven't got," he often said, whenever we'd want something.

"You get what you want and you find out it was not really what you wanted after all, and then you want what the *other* guy has," he'd warn, adding, "People need to find contentment with what they already have."

I also recall him telling the three of us kids about Ralph Waldo Emerson and his book, *Self Reliance*. He'd remind us, "Emerson said it best, 'Be careful of what you want, for you will surely get it.'"

My Dad's proverbial pearls of wisdom were unforgettable, and I found myself standing there in Barnes & Noble missing him all of a sudden, even though he was just a phone call away. One time I joked with my dad about marrying a woman who had big money, and I'll never forget how he quickly replied, "If you marry money, son, you're going to pay for it." Sage advice like this was *always* coming from my Pop, and I was blessed to have him.

These thoughts put me in a better mood within seconds, as I sat at the table waiting for Tommy to tire of the game. I knew it wouldn't be long, because it looked from a distance like Tommy's moment in the sun was clouding up fast, no doubt a result of the customers who had formed a lengthy line behind him. Those in line were leaning to their right and left, trying to see what was taking so long at the counter, and the young server couldn't help but feel their impatience.

"Let's get this 4th step written and then go to the Lenox Mall," Tommy enthusiastically suggested, as he sauntered up to my table.

"Nothing like a young woman flirting back with you to make an old guy like you bounce in his boots," I replied.

"Oh, I was just having a little fun," Tommy insisted.

"That's how it starts, grasshopper, a little fun — and then a *lot* of fun, and then feelings get involved, followed by all the chaos and devastation and an inpatient residential stay at TRC, remember?"

"Oh, how right you are, John. And I don't even *have* to remember. My wife, unfortunately, reminds me almost every night on the phone."

"Sorry to hear that, my friend. Hopefully she'll be able to forgive you one day. Ask her to check out these verses on forgiveness, Tommy, and —"

"No way, she doesn't want to hear *me* suggest *anything*. It would have to come from another source."

"Who does she respect among your mutual friends, or among her girlfriends, someone who actually *likes* you and won't mind being complicit with you in giving your wife what *you* want her to hear?" I asked him.

"You're devious, but I like it," Tommy replied. "I know a couple of mutual friends from our church and even from the office, who she'll listen to."

"Good. Give 'em these verses, because they're right on the

money. If she wants to be forgiven for what *she's* done in this life — and I'm sure she's done things in her past that she's not proud of — then she has *no choice* but to forgive you, according to Matthew 18:35 and these other verses. Here, give these to the person she trusts the most."

"Thanks man, I appreciate this. You really know the Bible, John."

"Yeah, well, if I could only practice what I preach, I wouldn't be here with you, my friend, now would I? There's another verse in the book of James, which tells me to be a 'doer of the word,' not just another idiot running their mouth about it. Basically, Tommy, I need to walk the walk more — and talk the talk less."

"Give yourself a break, John. You're way too hard on yourself. Let's have some fun, and go malling it at the Lenox, OK?"

"I thought you wanted to write our 4th step? That's why we came here."

"True, but if we troll the mall and meet some fralines, it'll give us even more juicy stuff to add to our 4th step!" He was howling at his own joke, and his contagious laughter had me going right along with him.

Going to the Lenox Mall with Tommy was a blast, at least until you realize just how much money you spent. Maybe that's the real reason I was redirecting him from the mall for a moment. Last time I went with Tommy to the Lenox Mall, I came back to TRC with a complete new wardrobe of expensive Tommy Bahama slacks and shirts, and some fine Italian leather shoes, looking almost as dapper as him. And that's saying a lot, because Tommy was the poster boy for GQ magazine, as debonair as they come.

Tall and handsome like me — OK, *more* handsome than me — Tommy was always dressed to the nines. He had those kind of soap opera, doctor good looks, the kind that make an otherwise unimpressed, proper and prudent woman do a double-take in public. Tommy was quick to charm just about anyone and everyone with whom he came into contact, and he could usually do it effortlessly, just by being himself. He was as smooth as water off a duck's back, conversant with anyone about almost any subject matter you might imagine.

"OK, we'll do it in reverse order; we'll write the 4th step and *then* go to the mall. We'll do it *all*," Tommy replied, with the kind of energy that a triple shot of espresso will give you.

"Besides, there are a million beautiful women at the mall, and how long's it going to take us to write down all the bad things we've ever done? I don't know about you, but I can't think of too many, so I'll be done in a few minutes," he joked.

"You're hilarious, Kimosabe. As for me, I'll be here till the cows come home. This 4th step requires us to list all our character defects, Tommy. And it says right here, we have to — 'do a fearless, searching moral inventory,' — and that means I have to list even *today's* character issues, like hanging out with *YOU*!

"Tommy, I agree that the mall's fun, but you, my friend, spend money like a drunken sailor. You're a big time urologist, so you can afford it; I can't. I'm only a lowly criminal defense lawyer, and though I deal with a lot of raw, naked truth in my business, *you* as a urologist are working up close and intimate with raw, naked guys *all* day long, so you're entitled to that big money!"

"Very funny," he mused.

"Hey, if I had guys coughing in my face every day from morning till night, I'd be popping pills too!" I joked.

"Now John," Tommy teased back, "it's just that sort of inappropriate humor that needs to be put on your 4th step list."

Within an hour, we were back at the mall doing what Tommy did best, flirting and spending money. He was right, we had a blast. And then on the way back to TRC, he agreed that he should immediately start a TRC "mall-doll, spendthrift support group for struggling urologists."

Chapter 15

Betrayal

I must have carried it around like a badge of honor, because Porter could tell I was still kicking the can about the whole betrayal thing. There had been plenty of opportunities to let go of it, but I just couldn't shake the whole reason I was here at TRC to begin with — Mike, the grow house, and the federal investigation.

"Why do you think you were such an easy mark for this guy, Mike, the marijuana grower?" asked Porter.

"I thought he was a friend, so I let my guard down," I replied.

We were sitting in the old man's cramped office, door shut and surrounded by the recovery slogans framed on his otherwise unremarkable walls. We were both drinking coffee like we used to drink wine, one cup after the other.

"You let your guard down because you have no guard, John. You — like most men who *live* to be liked by others — struggle with appropriate boundaries."

I just looked at him as if to say, "OK, go on."

"Like the rest of us who are guilty of people pleasing, you learn the hard way — like you're learning now. You trust *too* many *too* fast, you want to be accepted and liked by the masses, you violate appropriate boundaries, you get hurt, and then you cry betrayal. It's your own fault for being so needy, John."

"You make sense to me, Tom, because the whole betrayal thing has been happening more and more to me over the last couple years."

"Tell me about it" he prodded.

For the next hour or so we talked about the pain I had blocked for too long, specifically the Wainer ordeal.

"How did this other guy — what did you say his name was — *Wainer*? How did he hurt you?" he asked.

It spewed out of me like a faucet that couldn't be shut off. Porter was such a smart old man. He just sat back and listened as I told him the story that happened only a year or two before.

...

"'Can I have your keys?' David asked me."

Porter motioned for me to keep telling the story.

"Wainer said, 'I've got to put a present in your trunk for Elizabeth.' He said this so casually that I just reached and handed him my keys. We were across the table from one another at 'La Toretta,' a little Italian restaurant in Weston. I was too busy pouring over all the mail and bills that accumulated over the Christmas break to look up and thank him for being so thoughtful.

"It was now the first week of January and I hadn't paid any bills in over a month. My family and I had been on vacation for a few weeks and I hadn't seen the mail since before the holidays."

"Who was this guy, Wainer, and why were you meeting him?" asked Porter, letting me know I was going too fast.

"David Wainer was my assistant, paralegal, and I'll even say my friend. Our meeting was supposed to be uneventful, but it ended up being a night I would never forget."

"How so?" asked Porter.

"I remembered something at the table. 'Wait a minute,' I thought to myself, 'David never even asked me where I parked my car — so how's he going to put her present in the trunk, if he doesn't know where the car is parked? Besides, he didn't seem to be himself and he was acting guarded and shifty.' All of this gave me a check in my spirit that something was wrong."

"Go on."

"I said to myself, 'What's he up to?' There were hundreds

of cars parked in this very busy parking lot, so how in the world did he know *where* my car was parked, unless he had been there earlier casing out the parking lot? 'Did he watch me pull in, so he knew *exactly* where I had parked?' I asked myself. My thoughts were racing at that moment, and I remember that like it was yesterday, Tom."

"Go on."

"I felt scared for a second, out of nowhere. Now how in the world would I have intuitively known that I might have been in danger? Later I figured it had to be the Holy Spirit, as wild as that sounds. And I know you're looking at me kind of funny now — and thinking I'm getting all fundamentalist on you. Hey, I know this is beyond the curve for most folks, but as certain as I know my *name*, I *know* it was the Holy Spirit who physically *compelled* me to follow Wainer out of that restaurant. *He* certainly knew what Wainer was up to, even if *I* didn't."

"Where was the danger?" Porter asked, getting to the point.

"David knew that I kept a gun under the driver's seat. Something came over me — or again, I should say, *Someone* came over me — propelling me out of that seat and into the parking lot."

"Okay," Porter said.

"David had no idea that I was 30 or 40 yards behind him. My bizarre behavior is otherwise absolutely *inexplicable*, following him like that into the parking lot. I've never done that before, Tom, and I haven't done it since."

"Why did you trust this guy so much with your things?" Tom inquired.

I gave him a bit of my history with Wainer in an attempt to explain my level of trust.

"Elizabeth, the kids and I were skiing at Winter Place in West Virginia the week before, after spending Christmas with the family in Ohio. I remember asking David to go to the kids' school to retrieve their homework assignments and FedEx the homework to the ski resort; that way we could stay away longer than we'd planned.

"He may have even offered to do this, I don't remember, but we had done this before, as this had become a habit of ours. We never wanted the kids to fall behind in their schoolwork, simply because we were too undisciplined to end the vacation on time. We also got in the habit of asking David to buy groceries for Elizabeth's mother, who lives with us. We wanted to make sure she'd have plenty of food while we stayed away longer than we told her we would. David, our trusted 'friend,' was used to doing this for Elizabeth's mother."

"Yeah, you had *no* boundaries, John."

"Not just me. He was trusted by the kids' teachers to retrieve their homework, and he was appreciated and trusted by Elizabeth's mother, as well. Obviously, she was grateful for the man bearing gifts and goodies."

"They trusted him, John, because *you* trusted him."

"True, but our intentions were always good, for what that's worth. Even though I always paid him extra bonus money, perhaps he still resented doing the whole 'step and fetch' thing. We brought David into our family's inner sanctum, so if anybody knew our routines in life, it was David."

"That's not good when you're not dealing with immediate family or very close friends," Porter advised.

"I got to thinking that if he wanted to harm any of us, he knew exactly *where* to go and *when* to go there, to get it done. That's what made the parking lot scenario all the more frightening, especially when I thought about *why* it was he wanted to get into my car."

Chapter 16

Caught in the Act

"So was Wainer going for your gun?" Porter asked, getting into it.

"You would've *had* to have been there to really appreciate this, Tom."

"Oh, I can just imagine," Tom affirmed.

"David, my 'trusted' employee, opened the driver's door to my Lincoln Town Car. He had his back to me so he couldn't have known that I had watched him bend over and reach into my car.

"Jogging between the rows of cars in the parking lot, I recall slowing my step and my breathing as I approached his back. He was obviously not opening the trunk to leave a present for my wife; instead, he was retrieving something from under the driver's seat, where he *knew* I kept my gun. I had a semi-automatic .9 mm Glock."

"What were you *thinking*?" Tom asked, his face looking like it was *him* behind the car.

"My breathing stopped temporarily, and for some reason I remembered that the gun was loaded. Consumed by fear and anger, I screamed, 'What are you *doing*?'

"He abruptly stood up and started to cry. Without missing a beat, he tearfully told me about his girlfriend's former boyfriend threatening him; he was sobbing and whining something about, 'He's saying he's gonna cap me, John...I'm so scared...I don't know what I'm gonna do...I didn't wanna bother you about it...'

"I got in his face, yelling, 'You're telling me you didn't want to *bother* me?'... 'You idiot!'...'I would've thought that one of my kids got a hold of the gun.'...'Can you imagine how scared I would've been when I found it missing?'...'You stupid … ' I remember calling him every name in the book, Tom. To say the least, I was very angry. But I *now* know it was fear.

"Then I remember Wainer crying and repeatedly babbling, 'I'm sorry, I'm sorry, John, I wasn't thinking, please help me, I need help.

"Then I got up in his face again with, 'Why didn't you tell me or Malanga [our investigator] about this guy? Maybe we could have helped you. We could've run a check on this guy. Maybe he's got warrants out on him. You're gonna shoot somebody with *my* gun? You're a convicted felon! You get caught with that gun — you put yourself in possession of a *firearm* — *you*, a convicted felon — you're looking at 'possession of a firearm by a convicted felon,' a second-degree felony — and with your criminal history, you'd score *life*! That's real smart.'"

"'I know,' he mumbled, as he was crying, with his head hung down as he kept saying, 'I'm sorry. I'm so sorry; I wasn't thinking, please help me.'

"I put the gun in the car's glove compartment and locked it."

"Why did he want your gun?" Porter asked.

"*That* was the million dollar question, and on that night, at *that* time, he beat me again."

"How so?"

"It was just another layer of deception; only *this* time, he was leading me to believe that he had a genuine concern over *his* life, frightened about this 'former boyfriend.'

"It was life and death, all right, but I found out later it wasn't *his* life at stake. It's amazing, I later thought, that he had concocted this complete lie within milliseconds of being caught red-handed in the parking lot. And that's not bad when you consider the fact that he had less than a second to come up with it, from the time that I swore at him as he was bent over my driver's seat, to the time it took him to stand up."

"You believed him."

"Did I *really* think he was in trouble? It's hard to believe now, but yes, it's true; I bought his lie — hook, line and sinker. David, I learned, was *very, very* good at instant, *as well as,* premeditated deception."

What about Wainer's earlier victims?

Porter wanted to know more. "How long had you known this guy, and how did you meet him?"

"It is shamefully true that, *only* after catching him with my gun, did I even *think* about his prior victims and what terror they must have experienced when he stuck his shotgun in their faces."

"What?" Porter asked, rather stunned by the visual. "What shotgun, or victims?"

I proceeded to tell Porter the *whole* story of how I met Wainer as my client a decade earlier.

…

"He threatened and tormented them from behind his ski mask."

Porter helped me to recognize that Wainer's mask was symbolic of his whole personality. He still hid behind the façade of a gregarious charm and a gentle, helpful nature. His ski mask was obviously more apparent than the mask of his façade.

"'Those poor robbery victims,' I thought. Wainer had pushed these frightened, innocent young people into walk-in coolers. They had to have been terrified — mostly kids working part-time at night — scared they might die, worried about never seeing their families again. It made me feel all the more foolish for hiring him in the first place; and then again for believing his concocted story about his girlfriend's ex-boyfriend.

"I suppose I just *wanted* to believe that the nine years he had spent in prison had made him a different person, and that he was rehabilitated; but it could be, in retrospect, I might have had a hidden agenda when I originally hired him."

Porter helped me to see that I might have hired him — even if only subconsciously, to peddle him around as my "convicted felon" prop, to essentially prove to everyone my belief in redemption.

"You wanted to show the world what a *nice* guy you are," Porter suggested, smiling facetiously.

Then he wanted more of a backdrop, so I gave him the *entire* history.

Domino's, for a different kind of "dough"

"Before I knew Wainer, he had been convicted of robbing 11 Domino's Pizza and Sun Supermarket stores, all of them at gunpoint. He and his partner, a guy named Storts, committed the robberies throughout Broward and Palm Beach counties in 1987.

"When he was younger, Wainer had worked at Domino's Pizza, so he understood their franchise protocols including the peak times for the cash register drawer and where the safe was hidden behind the counter. But most importantly, he knew of their lax security: no cameras, no panic buttons, and only one landline phone located at the counter. All Domino's were — at *that* time, anyway — designed alike for cost efficiency; and they were basically run the same way, allowing Wainer to take advantage of that insider information.

"Wainer was represented by Jose Reyes, his Assistant Public Defender. He pled guilty to over a dozen armed robberies in 1987. David claimed that it was Jose, his attorney, who counseled him to admit to the robberies and throw himself on the mercy of the court.

"His *lawyer* told him to do that?" Porter asked in disbelief.

"In retrospect, I'm guessing it was *David's* idea, thinking he could get over on the judge and prosecutor and feign the requisite showing of contrition and remorse. Suffice it to say that *whoever* had the idea, it certainly didn't work. Judge Patti Henning hammered Wainer with a richly deserved sentence of 60 years — essentially a life sentence. He was looking at getting out at age 82, in the year 2047.

"Wainer was then determined to fight his 60-year sentence from inside his prison cell, and I was hired to help him do it. The assistant public defender, Jose Reyes, had a reputation for being a good man and a good lawyer, so attacking his competence and effectiveness would be a challenge.

"But it's fairly routine for a convicted inmate to throw his former lawyer under the bus on the grounds of 'ineffective assistance of counsel.' It's less often the case, however, that an 'indigent' defendant will claim to have no money for legal representation and *first* use a public defender, and then later in prison, miraculously 'find' the money to hire an experienced and private trial attorney.

"Old money"

"But unknown to Judge Henning and Jose Reyes and the public defender's office, Wainer's grandfather had a ton of money and owned an empire of real estate along Commercial Boulevard in Fort Lauderdale. Granddaddy predictably came up with his defense fund."

Porter and I then digressed into a tangential conversation about *why* the grandfather would invest in Wainer's cause. Porter suggested that perhaps the old man was just assuaging his conscience, throwing short money at these cases to *say* that he helped, so his family couldn't say he didn't.

"Maybe you're right; maybe he just threw some money at this thing to look good for the relatives," I agreed.

"It was either that, John, or your boy David was just *that* good at getting over on people. He must have simply fooled his grandfather too, just like he fooled you, your banker, and your accountant a decade later." The old recovering sage had him figured already.

Chapter 17

"Society Thanks You"

"How did you get this case — this guy Wainer?" asked Porter.

Porter and I made some more coffee together and refilled our cups. He wanted the "rest of the story," as Paul Harvey would say.

...

"The first time I met David Wainer was in 1987 in the Broward County jail. I had been there quite often to visit another client, Frankie, a wannabe wise guy, who happened to be Wainer's cellmate. Frankie had talked me up to David, who then talked me up to his grandfather. The family then hired me to handle the 'post-conviction relief proceedings,' to collaterally attack David's underlying convictions.

"Once hired, I set about to advance the theory that the guilty pleas should be set aside or vacated on the basis of the alleged 'ineffective assistance of counsel.' David helped a bit too, by 'snitching' or cooperating against his codefendant, Storts. We succeeded in first reducing the original 60-year sentence to 40 years, and then again to 30 years, then 27, 22, and ultimately, it was reduced yet again to 20 years — of which he served only nine!"

"Society thanks you for that, John," Porter joked, but then motioned for me to continue.

"But Tom, this 40-year sentence reduction consumed hundreds of hours of my life over two-years, sucking up to five different prosecutors and filing all kinds of motions. I essentially conned myself — as I often do — into believing that David was a decent guy, though he had done some very bad things. He appeared to be extremely remorseful and even repentant, as evidenced by his detailed, 87-page confession, or at least that's what I trumpeted to all five prosecutors," I explained rather defensively.

"Go on."

"Throughout his nine-year prison stint, we kept in touch often by writing letters to one another. In numerous letters, Wainer wrote very nice and seemingly heartfelt things, such as, 'I owe you my life,' and 'you and you alone turned my life around.' He also wrote, 'You're like a father to me.' He began ending letters with 'Love, David.' At the time, his letters encouraged me."

"It's unfortunate, John, and even a bit pathetic, I'm afraid, that you had such an insecurity and neediness at that time, don't you think?" asked Porter.

"Yes and no, and I'll tell you why — because David referred a few inmates to me as *paying* clients during his nine years away. After he betrayed me, I've asked myself, 'Was he resorting to 'self help,' believing he had some sort of referral fee coming to him for those earlier prison referrals?'

"The money was helpful when it came, and for that, I was grateful. He always claimed that he wanted to help me in the only way he could, so I took him at his word that he was a 'changed man' and that he felt he 'owed' me his life. When he began joking that he may work for me one day, I dismissed it as a humorous suggestion. But later, once I noticed how professional and intelligent he had become, his suggestion wasn't so absurd.

"'As a former cop and former inmate, he'd be perfect as a paralegal for my office,' I got to thinking. He could really help me and my clients, I figured, as he knew all too well from his own experience each side of the criminal justice system.

"He understood the loopholes and advantages of a complex prison system, the inside scoop on early release, good time, gain time, provisional credits, work release, parole, etc. I imagined a client saying, 'Hey, man, you don't understand what I'm going through,' and I could say, 'Oh, but we do. My own paralegal over there, David, has been just where you are, been there, done that. He's a convicted felon and he got a job.'"

"Looking back, I think you know that Wainer played you like a fiddle," Porter asserted. After nodding his head to punctuate his statement, he continued,"Though you say that you came to saving faith in Christ, John — and to be sure, that should've been *all* you needed for happiness, or identity and fulfillment — you often sought the approval and love of others. This struggle with insecurity, neediness and 'people-pleasing' is very real and very unhealthy. It can even be self-destructive, John, as it put you in a very bad predicament — one that risked your family's safety."

Redemption and second chances

"But wouldn't I be speaking out of both corners of my mouth, preaching redemption and the need to offer others a second chance on the one hand, while refusing to hire felons on the other?" I asked Porter.

Before he could answer, I added, "The average criminal defense attorney will go into court and argue for the 'second chance' scenario all day long, while never *giving that* second chance to a convicted felon with any sort of job within their own office."

"Are you saying that the average criminal defense attorney is insincere in making those second chance arguments in court?" he asked me.

He continued before I could answer.

"Or are they simply a little wiser from experience — or could it be that they don't struggle like you do with appropriate boundaries? Maybe they don't need to be liked by everyone?"

"In fairness to the truth," I replied, "I really wanted to *believe* that Wainer *was* the poster-boy for rehabilitation. And as a man of faith, I often speak of grace, mercy, forgiveness, redemption and 'a second chance, from the God of a second chance,' as my old pastor O.S. Hawkins would say. As a criminal defense lawyer *and* a man of faith, I thought that hiring a convicted felon would epitomize these biblical truths. I'd be putting my money where my mouth is, so to speak."

"You're conning yourself, John," he replied. "Oh, you're quick to give *God* the credit, of course, telling others that the 'God of a second chance' was giving your guy Wainer a second chance, while using this guy in the process to make *yourself* look good. Be honest. Might you have been making your own little provocative statement to everyone in your community?"

"You might be right."

Did I really hire Wainer to look like some sort of messianic figure myself, though giving lip service credit to God? It was true that I was getting Wainer cheaper than I'd ever get anybody else. There's no question that I proudly used him like a poster-boy prop, through whom I'd discuss all my favorite biblical truths and score points with clients.

I used him, I suppose, just as he used me.

Missing money

"John, getting back to this guy's intentions, what did he *really* want the gun for?" Porter pressed.

"That's the scariest part, from what I could figure," I replied.

"Let's have another cup and finish this pot of coffee, and tell me the rest of this story, OK? Porter suggested.

"Yes, another cup. This is one addiction I'm not giving up," I stated.

"Me neither," he replied.

He emptied the pot into our cups and sat back down, motioning me with his hand to continue where we'd left off.

. . .

"The day after I caught Wainer trying to get my gun, I was forced in a panic to realize that my life wasn't the same.

"My first day back in the office should've been calm; after all, I'd had a lengthy family vacation. But the phone rang at 8:30 in the morning. It was the bank. After less than a minute on the phone with the bank's Vice President, Debbie Block, I was in shock."

Then I gave Porter a real visual of what happened with the bank that day, recreating the whole scene for him:

"'Are you sure? How could this happen?' I demanded. Debbie was a friend, but I wasn't acting very friendly. 'Were there any big withdrawals lately?' I nervously asked.

Debbie's voice was calm. 'No, John. In fact, looking back through months of account activity, I don't see *any* large withdrawals at any time.'

"At this point I lowered my voice for fear that others in the office might hear. 'Then where the ... (sigh) ... where did all my money go?'

"'John, we checked and triple-checked everything. We consulted with our fraud division and there was no mistake made on our part. I'm sorry. I suggest you contact your CPA.'

"'You're telling me that I'm bouncing checks all over town. So, why am I just hearing about this now?'

"I was growing angry at her and at the bank, feeling that they were responsible for my problems. My frustration and anger turned to fear, when she filled me in a bit more.

"'John, we've been speaking with David in your office for a few weeks. He told us that you were aware of the problem, and you were in the process of rectifying it,' she said.

"My heart sank when she said Wainer's name. I suddenly felt ill. After that bizarre episode with my gun, and then the bank calling to say my account was overdrawn, my instincts told me to call the police. Another part of me — and I'm sure it was the whole pride thing — wanted to weasel my way out of this whole mess before embarrassing myself any further.

"Wainer's cell went to voicemail every time I called. He

didn't return my calls, and that's when I knew in my heart that he had betrayed me. The next person I called was my investigator, Larry Malanga. Larry and I planned for Wainer to come in and speak with us … to confess."

"Confess to stealing from you?" asked Porter.

"It goes beyond that," I continued.

"I began to wonder, 'Was Wainer going to do me with my own gun before I'd have the opportunity to discover the missing money? Was that his plan?' It really began to bother me."

"Now *that's* scary," Porter acknowledged.

"*Tell* me about it," I agreed.

"I then remembered that overwhelming Spirit-led feeling I had in the restaurant, when I told you the Holy Spirit launched me out of that seat. I'll always believe it was God saving my life, as melodramatic or crazy as that sounds. My compulsion to follow Wainer and intercept his theft of my gun, I'm afraid, was not just about stopping a gun theft; it was much, much bigger than that."

"No wonder you drink," Porter quipped.

He had me laughing out loud at that one, which made us both laugh for almost a minute.

Then he looked at me like he wanted me to finish the story. So I gathered my thoughts as to where I had left off and wrapped it up.

…

"The question was begged, 'Why did he need *MY* gun?' 'Of *all* guns on the planet, why *my* gun?' He could have protected himself with *any* gun — if just getting a gun was his limited intention; but what if he had more sinister plans, like killing me and making it look like suicide?

"And as a former cop, he would have known *exactly* how to make it look like a suicide. And it would have made perfect sense. You can almost hear the refrain around the courthouse community and all over town: 'Contini must've been depressed, or at the end of his rope. He was bouncing checks all over town, poor guy was broke and in trouble, couldn't support his kids, must've wanted his family to cash out on his life insurance policies,' you know the drill."

Chapter 18

"My Badge!"

"Did Wainer ever admit this to you, or to the police?" asked Porter.

"That's a whole story in itself, Tom."

Then I told it to him.

...

"Something else was bothering me, Tom, as I remember just sitting there in my law office thinking about Wainer being on the run and my financial plight and his betrayal, but I couldn't put my finger on it. My gaze continued to fall on a bare spot on my wall where a picture or a plaque had once hung. Then it hit me like a ton of bricks: *That's* where I hung my old prosecutor badge! The 'going away plaque' had my old badge displayed right on it. Did this scumbag thief have my badge too?

"My thoughts moved my lips as I said aloud, 'My badge too?' I was feeling real anger then — more than the hurt and fear I'd been feeling. *What* was he going to do with my badge? Why did he have to take that too? That plaque meant the world to me, along with the memory it brought to mind whenever I'd look at it.

"My old boss, Michael J. Satz, Broward's elected state attorney, always commanded my respect. Too many people *demand* respect, not knowing that respect is something to be commanded, not demanded. Mike Satz was very good to me, and I also had a lot of fond memories from my days as a prosecutor.

"And I'll never forget Satz presenting that plaque to me with my badge on it, right in front of the whole office during my ceremonious going away party. 'Wainer was robbing me of this too? That dirtbag!' I remember saying out loud. I was fuming!"

"What *was* he going to do with your badge?" Tom curiously inquired.

"That's how we eventually learned that other people would be in danger too, and that made it all the more important that I finally go to law enforcement.

"Wainer had been embezzling from me for over a year and a half, stealing more and more money over time. He had been forging one or two checks a week payable to himself, checks purportedly written by me.

"While I was away, he was intercepting the bank calls easily enough. But when I came back in town, he knew the party was over. He figured the bank would absolutely see to it that I knew my law office account was overdrawn. They would keep calling until they got their money, and he knew it. And he knew he could no longer intercept the calls now that I was home.

"His last chance to go undetected was *that* night in the parking lot — he knew I was still clueless when he asked for my keys. He was now in a panic, as evidenced by his behavior."

Conning the con?

"Thankfully, Larry Malanga, my investigator, first convinced him that I was harmless and that I *still* cared about him. He prevailed upon Wainer to meet me in the parking lot of the bank."

"That guy had to be good. We could use him up here at TRC," Porter joked.

"Malanga's style was almost always effective with people. He would almost invariably get people to trust him. He'd get everyone to open up with him, spilling their guts. Larry's countenance and affect were disarming, even to the veteran criminal.

"Wainer wouldn't look me in the eye. He was crying again right there in that bank parking lot, or at least I thought he was. It was becoming increasingly difficult to discern whether he was crying real tears from his heart, or whether he was just faking it like he did the night in the parking lot, as any sociopath could easily do.

"We talked Wainer into confessing to us, 'puking all over himself,' as we'd say in the business. Then we got him to spill his guts with Debbie Block, my banker, ostensibly for the purpose of educating the banker on all the 'clever' ways in which he beat the bank.

"'We need you to help us try to get the money back, David,' I told him, as he just hung his head. 'Look at me,' I demanded. 'Of course I'm deeply hurt over your betrayal, David, but right now I'm worried about the money and all my creditors, and you can help me now with *all* that, help to undo some of the damage you've created,' I continued.

"He was back to not looking at me, again with his head down, just like he was that fateful night at the other parking lot. I suppose this 'head hung low' thing, and the sheepish, defeated demeanor, along with the crocodile tears, must be right from the playbook on how to be a good sociopath."

"Now you're learning, John," encouraged Porter.

"How did you finish up with this "friend" of yours, the sociopath?" Porter asked.

Then I just recreated the rest of the speech I'd given David, to get him to cooperate.

. . .

"'Will you help me now, to minimize the harm?' I asked David.

"'Of course I will, John,' he replied, with as much sincerity as he could fake."

"These guys are good, John, and you can never let your guard down with them," Porter added.

"I hear you, Tom. In retrospect, his remarks about his willingness to help me reminds me now of that old saying — and it's probably the actual creed, if these sociopaths have one

— 'the secret to success is sincerity; when you can fake that, you've got it made.'

"Shame on me for being somewhat disingenuous, but I gave Wainer the same 'poor me, please help me' speech, with regard to my accountant, so he'd agree again to do the next right thing, as you're always saying, Tom. He then met with my accountant — who's now my *former* accountant — to explain in great detail how he was able to beat *him*, too.

"And that had to be hard for the accountant to just sit there by the computer and listen to Wainer, watching him demonstrate just how *easily* he got over on him. But I figured he had some of this humiliation coming to him, because he'd been sleeping at the wheel the whole time I was getting beat. 'He couldn't have cared about me at all,' I thought, 'because he didn't even insist on getting the canceled checks along with the monthly bank statements from Wainer.' My accountant's *inaction* almost *licensed* Wainer to hurt me, and not just me, but my whole family.

"Malanga and I convinced Wainer that we needed him to educate these professionals, if I were to *ever* have a hope for future restitution. 'Were we conning him?' I ask myself. Maybe, though not necessarily. We talked about how he might be able to find $10,000 or $20,000 himself, perhaps borrowing from family or friends; but we explained that we had hoped to achieve the *bulk* of the restitution from these other professional individuals and institutions, or their respective insurance carriers.

"These other professionals and institutions, we explained, had some real liability and exposure for allowing this to happen to me at all — or at least that was the speech *de jour* to get him to keep puking all over himself."

"Did he buy it?" asked Porter.

"He really had little choice, I suppose, because he figured he'd be arrested otherwise — and besides, he probably thought he was *that* good at conning me into believing he was *so* remorseful."

"No doubt," Porter agreed.

"But it's true; when I had Wainer running all over town publicly confessing to what he had done to me, I knew exactly what I was doing. He might've even *suspected* that I was building an airtight case against him, destroying any defenses he might have otherwise advanced, but that was a chance he was going to have to take.

"The more he confessed to others, the less chance he would *ever* have to successfully defend against a possible future prosecution. He was banking on his hope and prediction — he figured he knew me like a book — that I'd continue showing him my expected benevolence.

"He had heard my tired old speeches on mercy, grace and forgiveness — I can almost hear him mocking me as he's repeating my little refrains, followed by 'blah, blah, blah' — so he must have figured that he was quite safe in assuming I'd be just as predictable yet again. And, if his predictions were correct, he could then avoid the whole prosecution thing entirely.

"I'm guessing he truly believed I'd never actually follow through and have him arrested and prosecuted. He believed that I loved him on certain levels like a son and wouldn't want him sent back to prison. He was right, as I really didn't want that for him. This whole thing could've been resolved in a more benevolent way, if he had only demonstrated *true* contrition and repentance, perhaps by coming up with some money — $10,000 or $20,000 as even *partial* restitution. He claimed that he might have embezzled close to $50,000 over time.

"If he had just followed my directives, if he had come up with some money, if he had attended the counseling sessions with a pastor at my church, and if he had followed up with the psychologist, he would've been much better off."

"Oh, so you were going to play messianic figure *again* for this clown?" Porter asked incredulously. "You don't learn, do you?"

"I don't know what I was thinking; but then when he failed to attend the sessions with the pastor and the psychologist — coming up with squat for restitution — I began flirting with the idea of calling my law enforcement friends and having him prosecuted for just a few checks.

"I remember being straight up with Wainer and telling him, 'David, you *know* from all our cases that I'm friends with Detective Kevin Allen of the Fraud Unit of the Fort Lauderdale Police Department, and also with Scott Dressler, the lead prosecutor in the Economic Crime Unit (ECU) of the state attorney's office. These guys could easily fashion a *probationary* sentence of over 10 years, for example, with special conditions of probation that you pay restitution and undergo weekly counseling with a psychiatrist and counselor, and you can stay out of prison with the consent of the victim, me!'"

"Well, it's nice that you were forgiving the guy; but he's the wrong kind of guy to put on probation, I would think," said Porter.

"Unfortunately for Wainer, however, he ultimately underestimated my willingness and capacity to forgive."

Porter and I had to end our lengthy meeting in his office, as he had others to counsel. We agreed to meet later that day to finish the story.

Chapter 19

Truth or Consequences

Porter suggested we have a cup of coffee for a change. "I drink it all day, John, but whattayagonnado?"

"You and me both."

"Sit down and finish telling me about this character who betrayed you. But then when we're done with that, we're gonna teach you to quit playing victim, John. But for now, you got me interested in how this whole thing turned out. So tell me the rest of the story."

"Well, Wainer's prosecution was becoming more and more of a reality in my mind, since he wasn't coming up with any money.

"His actual sentencing was being structured in my head, or so I *thought*, but I was still tormented over the thought that he might have intended to kill me with my own firearm that night."

"Yeah, whatever happened with that?" muttered Porter.

"Well, I insisted that Wainer take a polygraph with this renowned polygraphist, Frank Carbone. Wainer was familiar with Carbone because I had hired him on many of my cases. Wainer agreed to the polygraph, I believe, because in his arrogance he felt he could *beat* Carbone, just as he beat the bank, my accountant, and me.

"But Wainer apparently underestimated Carbone, because he began flunking the test after two charts on the all-important question: 'Did you intend to harm Mr. Contini with his firearm?'

"And get this — David Wainer is the *only* person in my 20 years of experience as a former prosecutor and criminal defense lawyer who *knew enough* to walk out of a polygraph examination *before* the expiration of the third chart or test. He must have known as a former police officer that it takes three charts or tests before the polygraphist is able to state with any *real* certainty that a person was 'deceptive' or 'truthful' with respect to a certain question. After two charts, Wainer was perceptive enough to recognize by Carbone's otherwise subtle reactions or demeanor, that he was not passing the exam on this question."

"Wow," is all Porter said.

"Yeah, wow is right ... my 'thief' may have been much *more* than a thief that night, perhaps even a would-be *murderer*, because he was showing deception on the very issue of whether or not he intended to harm me with my firearm!

"He then tried 'Plan B,' I suppose, by coming up with another plausible reason why he wanted the gun, hoping to convince Carbone that he *never* intended to harm *me* with the gun.

"Wainer actually began confessing to Carbone that he was going to use the handgun to rob *other* people, as opposed to hurting me. 'Mr. Contini is like a father figure to me,' he told Carbone. He was pleading, 'I could never hurt Mr. Contini.'

"When Frank Carbone told me this later, I said, 'Father figure? That's puzzling, and maybe that's just because I never systematically embezzled $50,000 from my father.' Frank and I finally laughed a little."

"So this guy admitted he was gonna use the gun on other people, to convince the lie detector guy that he wasn't gonna kill *you*?" Porter asked, even more incredulous than he'd been before.

"Yes, he did, and by doing so — again hoping to convince Carbone that he would *never* have hurt *me* — he forgot that he was then essentially admitting that his entire earlier story about his girlfriend's former boyfriend was one big hoax. He basically showed us just how *quickly* he can lie convincingly under pressure.

"Even more importantly, Wainer was admitting that he was quite ready to threaten and harm *other* innocent people with loaded guns, after already serving prison time for similar offenses! He hadn't changed at all, even after doing nine years in prison for all of those earlier armed robberies!"

"Wow," was all Porter said once again.

"I know, he obviously didn't care about *anyone* other than himself. He was simply attempting to keep himself out of prison, by *any* means possible, and *that* was the reason I went to law enforcement. I could get past my *own* victimization on the money issues and deal with it on my own, but the violent, frightening robberies and victimization of *others*? No way, I couldn't get past that, because I owed a debt to my fellow man."

You can run, but you can't hide

"So what happened after that polygraph test?" Porter curiously inquired.

"Wainer took off running after he knew he was flunking Carbone's poly. Doug Dutko, a local bondsman, then helped me. Doug was a tough guy and a friend who I knew I could count on.

"Doug hooked me up with several other hired bounty hunters from the local bail bonds office. That same hour, I hired a half a dozen tough, savvy Haitian bondsmen, to surveil Wainer 24 hours a day, seven days a week, just in case he intended to come to my home or harm my family in any way.

"These Haitian guys would know exactly where Wainer was at all times. We could assist law enforcement in locating him when the time came to effectuate his arrest. Law enforcement needed time to get the arrest warrant drafted by an assigned prosecutor and then signed by a judge.

"None of that had been done yet, so Wainer couldn't be picked up; and, until he was under arrest, I was very uncomfortable not knowing *precisely* where he was at all times."

"I don't blame you," agreed Porter.

"My family and I moved into the Sheridan Hotel for three nights while my law enforcement friend from the Sunrise Police Department, Detective Steve Allen, kept his police cruiser outside my home.

"'What a true friend Steve Allen is,' I remember telling my wife. Steve went even further, agreeing to help Doug and the Haitian bounty hunters with police intelligence on Wainer's residence and other information.

"But as an ex-cop, Wainer knew he was being surveilled. This was quite obvious even to his pursuers, from all his elusive and evasive maneuverings. He frequently changed vehicles, entered through the backdoor of his lakefront townhouse, and circled the perimeter of the lake only at night, eventually beating the surveillance team."

"Now that's a scary guy — and a smart guy too," added Porter.

"True, but they kept hunting him. And it's also true that Wainer *was* winning, until Detective Sergeant Frank Miller of the Fort Lauderdale Police Department eventually hunted Wainer down like a dog and arrested him.

"Really?" Porter reacted, impressed as I was.

"Everyone called Sergeant Miller 'Frankie,' ever since my old days as a prosecutor. Frankie, a true friend like Steve Allen, had actually volunteered to help me. It wasn't even his case! He read in the newspaper that morning about Wainer being a fugitive and what he had done to me, so he swung by my office on his personal time to help me.

"He didn't just *offer* to help, which would have been nice enough; he just jumped right in and started getting his hands dirty when it wasn't even his responsibility. That's a *true* friend, under anybody's definition."

"That is a friend," Porter agreed.

"Frankie brought in the SWAT Team and the K9 unit, together with a dozen men under his command, to track down Wainer. Then, it was Frankie's idea to secure the cell phone 'site records' from Wainer's cell phone carrier. These records are not easy to get, not even for the police."

"Oh, really?" Porter reacted, rather surprised.

"Yeah, the cell phone carriers require a court order for customer privacy reasons.

"Frankie worked with my friend, Scott Dressler, the prosecutor, to secure the order from Judge Rothschild. Frankie knew *exactly* what Sprint, the cell phone carrier, wanted and needed in the court order, to avoid liability for releasing customer privacy information. So Frankie personally inserted all the appropriate language within the proposed court order itself.

"These cell phone site records enable law enforcement to know, within 12 city blocks, *precisely* where the caller is originating his cell phone calls, thereby placing Frankie Miller, his officers, the K-9 unit and the SWAT team within easy reach of Wainer — if only he'd use his cell phone.

"As it turned out, our brilliant little fugitive hadn't fled the area as suspected. Instead, he stayed near the downtown area and continued making cell phone calls.

"Frankie told us that by using the cell phone site tower information relayed by the cell provider, they tracked Wainer's location to a three-mile radius, then a two-mile radius, then one-mile, and finally they nailed him down to a 12-block area in Fort Lauderdale."

"It's neat that they can do that," stated Porter.

"Thank God. After hours of waiting for Wainer to make a move, they saw his SUV in motion. It cruised down a street right past them. They followed for a mile or so, and then pulled it over. The SUV stopped right away and Frankie told us that a young, petite black female sat scared in the driver's seat.

"'Where's David Wainer?' Frankie said he demanded from her.

"'I don't know,' she claimed. She identified herself as LaChandra, Wainer's girlfriend, who I knew as Ann Marie. After they kept questioning her — and I'm sure they threatened her with being an accomplice — she told them where to find Wainer. He was holed up in a reputed crack house. She confirmed that he was armed.

"Apparently, Wainer hadn't learned a thing from my speech that night in the parking lot when I reminded him of the fact that he was a convicted felon and could not be in possession of a firearm — a second-degree felony — or else he'd score tremendous prison time under the state's sentencing guidelines."

"Was he on drugs?" asked Porter.

"I don't think I'll ever know the *real* truth on that; but after some demands from the police, Wainer surrendered and came out. Frankie told me that he had a sad and defeated look of exhaustion, and yet also a strange look of relief on his face. Being on the run is tiring, both physically and mentally, I would imagine."

"You don't have to imagine, John, because you know what it feels like from real experience. Isn't that what you're doing here?"

"Touché, Tom."

"Go on," he said smiling.

"First let me recover from that low blow," I teased old man Porter back.

"At the police station, Wainer was allowed to make a phone call, and of *all* people, *who* do you think he calls?"

"Don't tell me he calls you," Porter guessed.

"You got it — he called the *very* person he betrayed. He

called me. That's obviously ironic, but I wasn't all that surprised, really."

"Neither am I, because he probably figured you'd give him yet *another* chance to get over on you!" laughed Porter.

"Yeah, you're right," I conceded.

"Did you ever get your badge back?" He asked.

"Yes, and really, that's a testament to the great police work performed by my friend, Frankie. Wainer didn't have it on him at the time of his arrest, but when Frankie later questioned him, he told him his buddy was keeping it for him. Frankie then called that guy and gave him assurances that nothing would happen to him if he'd just give me the badge back. They agreed to have the guy just leave it at a certain location for Frankie to pick it up.

"Sure enough, that guy did the right thing and Frankie got the badge and returned it to me. Aside from being a true friend, Detective Sergeant Frank Miller is one heck of a cop, to say the least — and to think that this wasn't even his assigned case."

"You owe that guy," Porter stated.

Chapter 20
Smell the Coffee

Porter and I spent the rest of the hour talking about Wainer's court outcome and sentencing, and what I learned from the whole ordeal. Porter listened, drank more coffee and kept me talking.

"I wasn't always warm and fuzzy or friendly with my friend, Scott Schirrman. In fact, I started off by threatening him, as he recalls.

"Personally, I don't recall grabbing him by his shirt collar and pushing him up against a wall in the courthouse, and yet he still insists that I did just that.

"It started when I was on my way to a courtroom within the halls of the courthouse. Schirrman walked up to me and introduced himself as Wainer's attorney. That was okay, until he began talking to me about Wainer's defense and the actual facts of the case.

"He asked, 'Did you, Mr. Contini, ever give David signature authority to sign your name on earlier occasions?' He was attempting to suck me into a conversation that could be used to benefit his client in the defense of his prosecution.

"Responding in a less than Christ-like fashion, I *do* recall threatening Scott with Florida Bar grievances and the possibility of his *own* prosecution. If my memory serves me right, I stopped him abruptly and spoke too closely into his face, 'violating appropriate boundaries' as you'd say here at TRC."

"We all do that too often," Porter suggested, throwing me a bone.

"Scott tells me today that I spoke to him in a very intimidating voice, getting way too close to him while staring into his eyes and calmly asking, 'Are you aware that I was the victim in this case, and not the opposing lawyer?'

"According to Scott, I threatened, 'And because I'm the victim, you're guilty of the second-degree felony of tampering with a state witness, which is something of tremendous interest to not only the prosecution, but also to the Florida Bar.'

"Scott claims that he was scared. My 'icy cold eyes,' he claimed, added to his concerns. He is considerably smaller than I am in stature, so when you add my angry comments to my 6 foot 3 inch frame and 225 pound presence, I'm sure he was justified in feeling threatened."

"No doubt," added Porter.

Shut up and plead guilty

"Within a week or so I lightened up on Schirrman, agreeing to assist his 'client,' so long as I was not put through any additional aggravation or stress by way of pretrial depositions or motions. He is quick to tell others today, that I was a man of my word, eventually speaking up in court on Wainer's behalf."

"There you go again," said Porter, shaking his head.

"But I made that deal with him for two reasons: to get him to hurry up and plead guilty, and because my faith dictates forgiveness — even if not necessarily for him and his sake — it's for *Christ's* sake and for *my* sake."

"Go on," he prodded.

"The sentencing transcript is clear that I kept up my end. I told Judge Paul Backman, 'I forgive David, your Honor; it's okay with me if the Court wants to allow for a downward departure sentence."

"What's that, John?" Tom queried.

"A 'downward departure sentence' means that the judge has the option of delivering a much lighter sentence so that the defendant gets many less years than he otherwise would score with his priors under the Florida Sentencing Guidelines.

"But Judge Backman instead approached sentencing from a strictly *legal* perspective — and one of real 'emotional sobriety,' as you guys say here at TRC."

"You ought to try it sometime, John. If you stop being a victim, you just might start enjoying your life, and enjoy some real peace," interrupted Porter, smiling at me.

"You know, you're a funny guy," I facetiously replied, smiling right back at him.

"Anyway, Judge Backman admonished David for quite some time before summarily sentencing him as a 'habitual offender.' His sentence meant that Wainer would receive no 'good time,' 'gain time,' 'provisional credits,' 'control release' or any other early release credit whatsoever, toward his prison sentence.

"Wainer's prison exposure in the separate economic crime case — the one involving me as the victim of various economic crimes — was of no real consequence compared to his prison exposure on the separate and unrelated second-degree felony charge of 'possession of a firearm by a convicted felon.'

"The charge involving the firearm was really indefensible, as he surrendered with the gun in his own back pocket! David was a repeat convicted felon and the firearm represented *huge* problems for him. So really, when he came out with that gun in his possession, his fate was sealed. No amount of benevolence or forgiveness from me could've persuaded Judge Backman to give him a pass on the gun possession charge."

"He must have wanted to go back to prison, from his actions," Porter theorized.

Sentencing

"His lawyer had nothing to argue for him, right?" Porter guessed.

"Schirrman went on and on for more than two hours at sentencing about Wainer's impoverished upbringing — with his own father in prison, about Wainer's alleged crack cocaine dependency, whatever spinning he managed to babble on about. He repeatedly suggested that 'Mr. Contini must have seen the good' in David Wainer, because Mr. Contini hired him *after* knowing full well all about his priors.'

"Scott did a great job with what he had. He can be quite an effective attorney, despite first impressions or appearances. He is not 'spit-and-polished' like some other trial lawyers; instead, he is rough-edged, and he's often disheveled — a lot of folks liken him to that 'Columbo' detective, the way he looks unkempt. Often he's repetitive, but he argues with real passion and a lot of heart.

"David then had only Schirrman in his corner. And Scott did a great job, but even if he had added a 'dream team' of lawyers, it wouldn't have helped. They had him dead to rights, and Backman was his judge. He had a ton of priors — and as a convicted felon a dozen times over, he surrendered with a gun on him! Backman was *never* gonna cut him a break; and truth be told, they were grasping at straws while hoping he would."

"How many years did the judge give him?" Porter asked curiously

"Thirty."

"Ouch."

Then I told Porter how the sentencing went down.

Chapter 21

Choices

"Judge Backman began his sentencing remarks with, 'Choices, Mr. Wainer — the three Rs: *respect for self*, *respect for others*, and *responsibility for your own actions*.' "The judge went on to remind him that the victim in this case, his own employer, had once worked tirelessly to get 40 years knocked off his earlier sentence; and if that were not enough, the same victim had given him his life back, providing him with a job, a cell phone, a decent salary, and *all* of the trappings of success, including a respectable identity within the courthouse community.

"Judge Paul Backman is an unassuming guy, but when he speaks in court you can hear a pin drop. His sentencing remarks were really memorable, but even though I remember them, I had my office fax them to me earlier today — to Diane at the front desk — in case you were interested in what Backman had to say."

"Interested? I'd *love* to hear his remarks," Porter enthusiastically offered.

"I thought you might want to read this sentencing transcript," I replied.

"Do you mind reading it *to* me, John, because these tired old eyes have been reading discharge papers all morning; but really, I'd love for you to read it, if you don't mind?"

"No sweat, here goes. This is Judge Backman:"

"Choices, Mr. Wainer. Everyone has choices. And when they make those choices they are responsible and accountable for what they do. You know, there are three R's that we learn in school: reading, writing and arithmetic. These are three R's that deal with life. It's something that you really ought to think about,

regarding everything that you have gone through, not only with this case, but also anything in your past as well.

"The three R's are the following: First is respect for self. Second is respect for others. And the last, probably just as important, is responsibility for all your actions. Those are the tenants by which we as individuals have to live.

"We make choices. Some are good. Some are bad. Just because a choice is bad doesn't necessarily mean that it has a significant consequence. But generally, every act has a consequence.

"In a sense, you have Mr. Contini in this courtroom, speaking well of you and exhibiting forgiveness truly from his heart. I have known Mr. Contini for quite a while. Words that emanate from him generally are not trite in any respect, and I would imagine the words he uttered in this courtroom today were probably some of the most difficult that he has ever had to do because he thought of you as a friend. He trusted you and you betrayed his trust.

"Whether or not he would have missed that money is irrelevant, because people in the position of trust, people in the position of authority shouldn't betray others.

"If you were a first time offender, I would sit here and I would tell you that everyone is entitled to mistakes. The question is: When we make a mistake, do we learn from those mistakes? If not, what does it take in order to establish that sense of responsibility that we have to have?

"We all have parents. Some of those parents are good, and some are not so good. Some of those parents are there for you, and some are not. Some, who are

physically present, still aren't parents in the sense that many of us would like. The fact is that your grandmother raised you; at least you had an individual there that was caring and concerned, who tried to do the best that she could.

"Mr. Wainer, you are not an individual who lacks education. You are not an individual who lacks intelligence.

"Having a dream, pursuing that dream, and then throwing it all away is something that you have to look at inwardly in order to determine why you did it. As a police officer, your conduct is absolutely reprehensible. You wouldn't tolerate this from someone you were going out to investigate and arrest. The fact that you only lasted in that position for a short period of time is something that you have to look at and make a determination as to where you went wrong. Could you have made this a career? And you messed up. You messed up real bad and you will pay that price.

"I am not going to diminish the fact that you were sentenced to a significant period of time in the Florida State Prison system. You had a very good lawyer who came in and was able to get it modified and reduced. The mere fact that you served less than ten years of a 20 year sentence — well, that's our system.

"You had the opportunity through the good heart and good graces of Mr. Contini to resurrect everything that life held dear for you. He understood your past. He knew you probably as well and maybe better than anyone else in your life at that time. He gave you a chance, an opportunity. He didn't give you menial labor. He gave you responsibility, and what do you do? You become a common thief, perpetrating a fraud, perpetrating a lie, living with it and then turning around

and blaming it on drugs.

"We all have problems. We all have to deal with those problems. It's not always our mothers and fathers that are responsible. No one can make you change, you either have that inside you or you don't.

"Now, I have heard a lot of rhetoric that's been stated here in this courtroom in the three and a half hours that we have been going through this sentencing. As I stated to you before you started to speak, the amount of time that you took is really of no consequence. That is what I am paid to do. I am here to listen; I am here to make decisions and to act responsibly on behalf of the citizens of Broward County. Whether it took us ten minutes or ten hours to do that, I would have sat here very patiently. I would have listened to everything you had to say, and everything Mr. Contini, your father, and your lawyer had to say.

"I dare say for a lawyer who doesn't portray himself as being in the upper echelons, your lawyer did his entire presentation on your behalf without notes, very competently, very eloquently and argued your position. He did a great job. I think he thinks less of himself than his abilities really show. But that's okay, because we all aspire to be a little bit better than we think we are. I think he did an extremely good job portraying the type of individual that he sees.

"Your lawyer filed a motion for a downward departure. And I have had the opportunity during the break to read the entire motion, all of the attachments, the case law that you have stated to me. I am certainly familiar with it, but I took the opportunity to once again review each and every one of those cases that you set forth.

"I have heard Mr. Contini's indication as to what he

believed, and the fact that basically he is leaving the sentencing in the hands of this court; and whether I depart or I don't depart he has absolutely no issue with.

"One thing I do want to clear up, deals with the issue of restitution. I take it — from all the statements that Mr. Wainer has said, both on the record and in the investigation and statements by the state and the police — that he doesn't dispute the fact that restitution is due. Mr. Contini has indicated that he is willing to cap the restitution at $50,000. And Mr. Contini is in the back of the courtroom at the request of the defense; he is shaking his head in the affirmative, agreeing with that.

...

"Mr. Schirrman, there is no question that the imposition of habitual offender sentence is one that is permissive and discretionary, not mandatory. Obviously, when the state files its notice of intent to seek habitual offender status of an individual under Florida Statutes, one of the main criteria that a Court today is faced with is, when a Court does not impose a habitual offender sentence upon an individual, the Court in writing has to explain why that individual is not a danger to the community.

"Now a danger to the community can be defined in many different ways. Certainly, if I look at the record of Mr. Wainer with nine armed robberies, correct that to ten, the seven kidnappings, and the one grand theft auto and two grand thefts, four aggravated assaults, the possession of a firearm by a convicted felon, in addition to the primary cases here, I dare say there is ground enough right there to say here's an individual who is a threat to the community, especially when he's got a prior CCF and he is being convicted again for the charge of CCF and carrying a concealed firearm by a convicted felon.

"*That, of course, leaves the Court in a decision-making process. Mr. Wainer, you are finished. Granted, he didn't use his gun, and certainly I have heard the explanation of what he was going to do. The fact remains that he still had in his possession a firearm, and that is dangerous.*

"*More importantly, it is a problem when an individual steals thousands of dollars from a trusted friend; you claim it happens every moment in corporate America. Well, I have seen an awful lot of individuals in corporate America that have been charged, and those individuals are doing some very significant prison time for effectively ripping off the public. So when they are charged, many do fall. And I dare say, many of them aren't sitting there already with 24 prior felony convictions. That's an awful lot. No matter whether you are a lawyer or an accountant, 24 prior felonies are a lot. And these are significant.*

"*The fact remains that when you consider those matters that you have asked me to consider on your motion for downward departure, while many may, in fact, exist, those two are discretionary with the Court, as to whether or not the Court wishes to utilize those as a basis to depart.*

....

"*Wainer was a former police officer and may get sentenced to places where hostile individuals that he knows might be; those are consequences of choices. He knew what he was looking at when he perpetrated this crime.*

"*Your request for a downward departure, all things being taken into consideration at this time, is going to be denied.*

"*I would find Mr. Wainer was served in open court*

with a notice to declare him a habitual felony offender. I would find that the necessary certified copies of convictions have been placed upon the record, that they have not been set aside in any post-conviction proceeding, reversed on appeal, nor has he been pardoned by the governor, and that he does otherwise qualify for habitual treatment under Florida law.

"Accordingly, at this time, with regard to case number 99-4015CF10, on the grand theft in the second degree, the Court is going to adjudicate the defendant guilty, impose a sentence of 30 years Florida State Prison as a habitual offender with credit for 117 days, impose restitution in the amount of $50,000.

"As for case 99-5129 on the possession of a firearm by a convicted felon, that's an adjudication again, 30 years Florida State Prison with credit for 117 days. Also, five years as a habitual offender. In both cases, all counts run concurrent.

"Mr. Wainer, Mr. Contini may forgive you, but I don't."

"The judge's allocution was wonderful and very real, and it was impossible to contest," I said.

"Good," Porter volunteered.

"You're right; in retrospect, most people would *champion* the fact that the judge gave Wainer a 30-year sentence, considering his criminal history of a dozen or so armed robberies.

"The judge apparently saw Wainer as a sociopath who had no remorse for his earlier violent crimes. He saw *beyond* all the testimony of forgiveness and all the things I wanted to talk about, and instead, he saw all those earlier victims who were placed in coolers with shotguns stuck in their faces.

"Backman saw the potential for future victims once Wainer obtained his new badge and firearm. The judge reasoned that it took a unique individual to betray the very lawyer who helped him get out of prison. And even though I was very public when I testified to forgiving David —"

"John, I need to interrupt you here. Are you sure you weren't just using this Wainer character *again* as a prop of sorts — like you did when you hired him initially — to show off your whole faith and forgiveness thing?" Porter inquired, rather astutely.

"Maybe you're right, Tom. I never really thought it through quite like that — maybe that's actually true on certain levels."

"But the best part of my testimony was the fact that I actually *meant* everything I said, at least *when* I said it. Sometimes I go back and forth on this *now*, especially when I consider the financial *nightmare* that *Wainer* caused me. His actions precipitated my slide down that slippery financial slope, to my feeling a bit desperate — and even to my most recent stupidity — trusting this guy Mike who wore a wire on me. And all that led me here!"

"You're playing victim again," Porter chided.

"I'm just saying why unforgiveness can at times rear its ugly head again — when I think that it was *Wainer* who initially put me in this financial soup so *deep* — and then I let my guard down with Mike, my contractor friend, who turned out to be this marijuana grower — and then *he* betrayed me too."

"It's not about Wainer, John, and it's not about this clown, Mike; it's about *you*."

I just stared at him because we both knew he was right.

"These things are happening to *you*, John, *because* of you. You were too needy, and yes, insecure. People pleasing can be very destructive, John. You do things to impress others and you lose your true self in the process. You think you're using these guys, but it's *you* who's being used. That's what happens when you don't have appropriate boundaries. These guys are just these guys; next year it'll be two other guys. They didn't do this to you — *you* did this to you. Your best thinking got you here."

This old man was so smart, that all I could do was look down and slowly nod my head.

"When you're right, you're right," I finally said, looking up at him, feeling almost emotional.

Our meeting in his office was over. We both knew that all that needed to be said, was said. He stood up and came around the desk and opened his arms to invite a hug. We hugged for what seemed like a minute, though it wasn't that long. He knew, as did I, that he had helped me.

Chapter 22

"Don't Leave Before the Miracle."

All along, I had been in communication with Mike Dutko, my lawyer friend in South Florida. By the way, there are few lawyers in the same league as Dutko, and even fewer more respected by prosecutors. Dutko had been speaking with the assigned federal prosecutor in the U.S. attorney's office, regarding my exposure in their investigation.

Toward the latter half of my stay at TRC, the prosecutor said something to Dutko I'll never forget:

"I don't know whose idea it was to get Contini out of town when you did, but it was the smartest thing he ever did."

Of course, in my flesh, *I* wanted to take credit for that idea, but it was in my *spirit* that I had felt the need to flee. Right or wrong, I'll always believe it was the Holy Spirit's idea. *He* had me flee, or He at least made me feel the need so overwhelmingly that I acted on it.

The federal prosecutor told Dutko that he was actually dropping the investigation. He even added that he wished me well in my recovery efforts. He agreed that my former client, his witness, was *not* credible. He had apparently destroyed whatever credibility he had left with the involved agents when they caught him lying about others.

He had been given enough rope to maneuver against other "targets" after my abrupt departure, and predictably, he had "hung" himself with a number of inconsistencies. As Providence would have it, I was no longer in danger of indictment at home.

It was then that I remembered what Nanci Stockwell and Thurmon Strother had said throughout these months: "Don't leave before the miracle." But was this a miracle, the fact that the federal thing was going away? Maybe, but one thing I knew for sure in my spirit: the God of a second chance was working out something big for me and my family, one way or another.

Overwhelmed by the realization that a miracle was really happening in my life, I immediately wrote letters to my parents.

Pop,

Elizabeth may have told you already — but even if she has, she may have left out quite a bit. My lawyer and friend, Mike Dutko, confirmed the fact that the feds "were" (hopefully past tense!) looking at me pretty hard. I'm hopeful that much of this is already behind me, though we cannot be entirely sure. Getting outa dodge could not have happened at a later time.

It does appear as though my absence has frustrated the agents' efforts in targeting me on certain issues. They were, in fact, monitoring my phone conversations; and though it's unlikely to have continued for the three months that I have been gone, it may still be a possibility.

I'm working with Dutko to get the necessary closure on this, so please understand my reluctance to openly discuss over the phone what led me here to TRC.

...

There's nothing about those earlier mistakes which I can change now. My lawyer has done a good job in speaking with the substitute counsel for these guys, and in humanizing me with the federal prosecutor; but one thing is clear — I certainly got out of that case and out of town just in time.

Pop, I'm praying throughout the days here for my family, and whatever the outcome, I'm making changes in my life upon my return. I intend to manage more and not micromanage — and if I'm blessed with extra income, I'll get into the personal injury business where it's safer and more lucrative — and where I can still help the little guy against the greedy corporate slobs who otherwise take advantage.

Anyway, I intend to make other personal life changes too, e.g., to slow way down and take on less activity, to abstain from drinking and doing other destructive things. I'm excited about an entirely new season in life.

I think about you all the time and I'm praying for you guys too. I'm sorry if I disappointed and worried you. ... I'm now beginning to understand why I did what I did.

Elizabeth has been wonderful, and she has held the family together. I speak with them almost daily, and we did get to spend about a week together two weeks ago in Atlanta. We had some great times.

I've been thinking, Pop, that maybe there is something to this hypomania thing after all, though the docs here disagree with each other as to whether or not I'm hypomanic on certain levels. One says yes, one says no, another is clueless — this forensic stuff is anything BUT science, in my opinion; and if we're ever looking for diagnostic certainty, it's not with shrinks and forensic psychologists! ... But regardless, right or wrong, I'm running with it if it helps me with the legal, etc. The brutal truth is: I'm probably no more hypomanic or bipolar than most nut case trial lawyers, according to most of these folks; but these feds don't care about truth — they'd just love to take down a lawyer, period.

I've been getting in trouble all my life. Even you used to say, "They're gonna make you President someday, or they're gonna hang you." Hey, did you know that Einstein and Churchill were both bipolar? So were

Abraham Lincoln (they called it manic depression), Theodore Roosevelt, Ted Turner, Francis Ford Coppola, and the list goes on. So even if I 'legitimately' had that diagnosis — which I don't — at least I'd be in good company!

I'm amazed that my faith by itself was not enough to keep me in check, against my disobedience. Before I came here, I felt like such a hypocrite and a fraud. I was going to two Bible studies a week, regularly attending church, and memorizing over a hundred relevant Scriptures. You'd think that would be enough. I remember being in Israel in His empty tomb, the Garden of Gethsemane and on the water @ the Sea of Galilee, getting baptized in the Jordan River (right where Christ was baptized!), and I even went down into the dungeon @ Caiaphas's house (where they threw Jesus after His arrest in the Garden of Gethsemane, right before His trip to Pilate's Praetorium) ... And with all these visuals and experiential feelings and heartfelt beliefs and wonderful Scriptures in my head, I still couldn't bring myself to stop sinning and stay obedient.

That's why I like Psalm 23: "The Lord is my Shepherd"... "He makes me lie down in green pastures."... He MAKES me. I wouldn't lie down long enough to stop hurting myself and those around me, so He is MAKING me lie down right here in Atlanta.

I also like that prodigal son parable that Jesus told in the 15th chapter of Luke. That story is a wonderful word picture for me, as Jesus describes what the Heavenly Father is really like — how we can (and do) turn our back on Him, and yet He doesn't turn His back on us; and we can "come to our senses" and smell the coffee, wake up and come back to our Father.

Pop, I feel like that prodigal son slowly coming

home, with our Heavenly Father running out to this field in Atlanta to greet me "with outstretched arms.

Cool, huh? And I also like Hebrews 12:6-10, as He explains that God disciplines those He loves...going on to explain that this discipline or punishment is evidence of the fact that we're loved as His children; and I remember He uses the words "correct" and "chastise" too, along with "discipline."

Just like you corrected and chastised and disciplined us as kids — precisely because you loved us, and just as I discipline or correct my kids (so others will love them; or to prevent them from getting hurt!) — it's cool to think that God disciplines those of us who consider Him as their Father, again because He loves us. Anyway, bottom line, I know I'm loved, by you as my earthly Pop and by my Heavenly Father too!

Please give Marta and Anthony a big hug, and please take good care of yourself, OK? I love you very, very much. You're a wonderful father, like the father in the 15th chapter of Luke. (Re-read that chapter; you'll like it again). Please eat veggies, lay off the milk, bread & desserts, and walk more for exercise, OK? I want you around for a long, long time!

Love, John

P.S. Sorry about the unsolicited advice from drug camp!

Dear Mom,

It was wonderful talking with you last night. I'm so grateful you're safely back home in Portsmouth from Ireland. I'm happy that Kathleen, Elizabeth & Donald kept my confidences and honored my request that you know nothing about my purposes in Atlanta until after you returned from Ireland. I did not want to affect your trip-of-a-lifetime in Ireland or cause you to worry about me while you were hopefully enjoying yourself over there.

Your trip reminds me of the great times we had traveling together. You're so much fun to travel with; I especially enjoyed it when we traveled to Ireland together with Elizabeth. You were a blast, so much fun and lots of laughs! It was also a real special treat to have you in Israel with us — all throughout the Holy Land! Remember being on the Sea of Galilee on the little "disciple boat" together? The singing, with O.S. preaching a sermon, your tears captured on my video camera! You remember me kiddingly threatening that you'd better pray to receive Christ (again!), or else I'd throw you over the boat?

You're a real trooper, Mom. Remember getting dunked by Dr. Criswell (the 80 year old man) & O.S. in the Jordan River, baptized publicly just like Jesus did in the same river? Cool, huh? Your Heavenly Father was smiling big time on His little daughter, Noreen. You are one of His biggest saints, Mama. Do you know that?

Being alone here at TRC makes me remember and really appreciate you. We always had a great, loving, warm and supportive relationship. You were <u>always</u> very encouraging, loving & nurturing! I don't regret any part of our history & relationship together. I don't recall any mistakes you may have made in raising me; and in fact, I recall you making no such mistakes. You & dad may have made some mistakes w/one another (and I'm not thinking of anything in particular), but you didn't err w/us!

I'm blessed to have the world's greatest & sweetest and most loveable, well-liked, caring & compassionate mom. I know this. God was smiling on me big time when

He blessed me with you. He blessed me with a <u>wonderful</u> family. And yes, of course, I wish that the divorce never happened; but I suppose I still need to pray: "God grant me the serenity to <u>accept</u> the things <u>we cannot change</u>, the courage to change the things we can, and the wisdom to know the difference."

It's been over 29 years since your divorce, and we kids have all done very well. There are countless people who have been denied a good mother or a good father, who have suffered abusive upbringings, poverty, disease, etc. We need to look at our glass as being <u>more</u> than half-full, and not with the half-empty mentality. All in all the situation forced all of us to experience growth; and we all had to experience what we did for reasons known only to God.

My biggest, most frequent thought about my childhood is that I'm blessed to have had such a wonderful childhood. I do wish that I had more memories before the age of 6. Maybe with longer sobriety I'll remember more, huh? I wrote Pop the attached lengthy letter. Rather than repeat a lot of what's contained in that letter, I thought I'd just send a copy along to you. This way, you're brought up-to-speed on the issues, re: my work, the investigation, my lawyer, etc.

I've definitely benefited by being here, even as I "thought" I'd played the docs and the feds like a fiddle for awhile. I got over on everyone for the time it took to get "out of the woods" — or so I thought, but I apparently also got over on myself. And it's kind of funny that God could use my own disingenuousness to get me the help that He knew, in His omniscience, I really needed.

Mom, I'm thinking of making many changes in my

life — possibly even a vocational change (or addition) as well. I'll fill you in more when I see you, OK? If I stay doing the lawyer gig, I'll hire another lawyer to take on more cases, allowing me to go down the road & do some more fun things.

Possibly you and Elizabeth & the kids can get together soon after you get rest — or maybe we can meet you in Portsmouth when I leave Atlanta.

I love you <u>very, very</u> much, Mom, and I'm praying that you continue to stay in that 'new Noreen' phase of adventuresome activity, daily walking, healthy eating, etc.

We can never grow too spiritual or too connected with God, so keep going with your growth there too, OK? I'll call soon.

Love, your John Patrick

Chapter 23

The Preacher and the Burglar

It was another beautiful sunny summer afternoon at TRC. I was hanging out on that soft green grass, enjoying the breeze and getting some sun while thanking God for my redemption and second chance.

Just then, I thought of another man who had been blessed with the same redemptive second chance. Thankfully, I'd had the pleasure of representing Scott just a year earlier, and only now that I had an attitude of gratitude, could I fully appreciate my involvement in his life and what had happened with him. Everything was clearer now.

What are the odds that someone would burglarize a preacher's home and then end up being represented by the preacher's friend, a criminal defense attorney? Those odds are astronomical, at best; and yet that is precisely what happened in young Scott's life.

Scott, whose surname I withheld to protect his identity, was arrested for burglarizing the home of Pastor Larry and Cynthia Thompson. At an appropriate time much later, Pastor Thompson was moved to share this true story from the pulpit. He was preaching a sermon on forgiveness and grace, weaving in the biblical examples of Jesus forgiving the guilty criminal on the cross next to Him, while also forgiving His own murderers — the very individuals who were crucifying Him. It was in *this* context that he told the story of how he forgave the young man who burglarized his home.

Lying there on the grass by myself, I found myself laughing. Anyone walking by would've thought I needed to stay a *lot* longer at TRC! But I could've cared less as I was just enjoying myself while reflecting on what Pastor Larry had told the church. He had the congregation laughing hard a few times, as he explained how he went into a big time panic and ran upstairs to the bedroom, warning his wife, "Wake up and get out of bed! There's a burglar in the house!"

He shared the fact that his wife didn't believe him. She was said to have replied, "You *always* hear people in the house."

But this time Larry *knew* there was someone in the house, because he actually *saw* the individual peering into the sliding glass doors. He then heard the door open, just before he bolted up the steps to the bedroom.

The preacher got on the phone, dialed 911, and tried telling the dispatcher all about the burglar, only to then be interrupted by the dispatcher's questions, "Do you have a dog? And do you have a gun?"

The way he told the story with *real* animation from the pulpit was hilarious, probably because he made us *feel* the tension — as though *we* were in that house with a burglar — responding to those questions from the dispatcher under that pressure, at that time!

He explained that he told the woman on the phone that he had a Shitzu — a dog too small to intimidate *anyone* — and that he had an antique rifle with no bullets. He created quite the visual from that pulpit, causing all of us to just *imagine* the horror of having someone in their house, and yet we were howling at some of the comical exchanges occurring on the phone with the dispatcher, and better yet, between Larry and his disbelieving wife.

The next thing the preacher and his wife heard were two officers, crouched outside the sliding glass door, screaming, "Don't move or I'll blow your head off!" The pastor told us he cleaned up the officers' language so he could share the story from the pulpit. We could all imagine how the officers *really* communicated their admonitions.

The dispatcher was keeping Larry calm over the phone, telling him that the officers were outside the house waiting for backup. The way Larry tells it, he was panicking and desperately begging the dispatcher to tell the officers to get on into the house *now*, and *not* to wait for backup; because after all, the burglar was already in the house! He was recreating his level of panic from the pulpit, and though it was as serious as a heart attack that night, it was funny in church the way he told it.

A few more moments passed and then the pastor and his wife could hear the officers shouting at the burglar downstairs.

"Mr. Thompson, the suspect is now apprehended. An officer will be coming up the stairs to your bedroom. It will be the officer at the door and not the suspect," said the dispatcher.

"Thank God," replied Pastor Thompson and his wife Cynthia, in unison.

When they opened the door for the officer, he showed them identification from the suspect's wallet, and asked them, "Do you recognize or know the suspect?"

Larry told the officer that he did *not* know the suspect. But then he shared with all of us what *Cynthia* had to say when *she* was shown the wallet identification.

She quickly said, "Look, Larry; he has a movie watcher's card *just* like us," which caused about 3,000 of us in church that morning to laugh wildly.

The preacher went on to tell the congregation of a defense lawyer in church, referring to me, whom he had asked to go with him to speak with the burglar.

"Let's go to jail!"

Pastor Larry wanted to go down to the jail and visit with the burglar, curious as to *why* he had come into his house. In addition, Larry hoped that he might possibly have the opportunity to share the gospel with the young man.

I admonished the preacher not to meet with the burglar yet. I felt concerned, because I had learned that their daughter,

Jennifer, was home alone for a few days before Larry and Cynthia returned from vacation, just before this burglary. At this point we didn't know *why* the young man was in the house. Perhaps he was casing out the house and was stalking Jennifer, not interested in any kind of theft at all. Since the burglar's intentions were still unknown, I suggested to Larry that it would be better if my investigator and I established the *initial* contact with the young man.

"We need to determine *what* his intentions were when he broke into your home, to make sure it didn't have anything to do with Jennifer," I explained. "Pastor, I think it would be better for you to meet him a little later, after we know what he was doing there."

Pastor Thompson agreed, saying, "Wow, I didn't even think of that, John. Boy, you have to think like that in your business, don't you?"

"Another reason not to see this guy alone," I explained to the pastor, "is the fact that he would then learn that you're a sweet-spirited pastor, most likely not inclined to use a firearm in the future. Had he been after Jennifer, or if he were thinking of making another attempt to get into your house, he would know that he was not walking into harm's way."

"OK, John," the pastor replied, "you'll see him in jail first. And then when you think the time is right, I'd really like to talk with the young man. Perhaps we can help him."

The pastor's heart was so pure, I thought, unlike mine on this one. I'd have to be careful to admonish the young man that I was *not* there as *his* attorney — meeting him unsolicited like that in the jail. Instead, I'd have to make it clear that I was attempting to play the role of mediator between him and the involved victims in this case. If the young man had already secured the services of an attorney, I'd reach out to his attorney.

It was all coming back to me as I stretched out on that lawn at TRC. I couldn't believe how my memory was replaying this case as though it were yesterday, and I was seeing things I hadn't noticed so clearly before.

When I checked on the defendant in the jail records, he had already bonded out within 48 hours of his arrest. "Someone loves this guy," I told the pastor, "because most burglars don't have the money to bond out. That's why they typically break into houses and businesses, to get the money they don't have. Whoever bonded him out will know where he is; and if it's his family, then he might even be at the same address as whoever posted the bond."

"Your worst nightmare or the best thing that ever happened to you!"

My investigator, Larry Malanga — about the best in the business — was a big guy who made me look petite. He was one of those guys who, if he didn't take measures to minimize or soften his appearance by stepping back a bit and being extra polite, he could be intimidating; and yet in most cases, Malanga would "polite" the people to death and surprisingly get all the information he needed, stuff nobody else would get.

Together we went to the defendant's home and knocked on the door. Even though no one answered the door, we knew there were individuals inside as we heard noises and there were several cars in the driveway. Before we left, we made sure the individuals inside knew we were coming back.

Then we spoke to the immediate neighbors and learned that the defendant had a cousin who lived in a house nearby. So we walked over to that house and spoke to the cousin, making it very clear that we were *only* interested in knowing *why* his cousin was in the home; we also made it very clear that we needed to communicate with Scott.

We had earlier learned that Scott was on probation for a prior DUI offense. Right or wrong, we informed his cousin that this recent burglary arrest was a violation of that earlier DUI probation, something we believed would be of real interest to Scott's probation officer.

That was our leverage.

We went on to inform the cousin, "We'll recommend to Scott's probation officer, and then to the assigned judge, that Scott should receive the maximum sentence allowable by law on his violation of probation offense — 364 days in the Broward County jail; but should Scott be willing to *assist* us and somehow convince us that he had *no* intention whatsoever of harming anyone in the Thompson home, we *could* be the *best* thing that ever happened to him."

His cousin was definitely paying attention now.

"Perhaps we could recommend benevolence and possibly even a dismissal of the burglary prosecution itself," we explained, "with additional benevolence on the violation of probation sentence."

Within 24 hours of our little "legalized-extortion" speech (it's legal, as law enforcement does it all day long!), I received a phone call from Scott, and we arranged to meet at the Rainbow Diner down the street from his home. After my initial conversation with Scott, I arranged for Pastor Thompson to join me at the Rainbow Diner for the prearranged meeting.

Chapter 24

"Second Chances!"

Before the meeting, we had researched and learned background information about Scott. From documents cross-referenced with Scott's date of birth, we learned the identity of the assigned judge and prosecutor. The assigned prosecutor was coincidentally a friend of mine, Sharon Mullane, who I *knew* would listen to reason. Interestingly enough, Sharon was a professed Christian too, with a strong sense of fundamental fairness and objectivity.

Scott was a college student and a cheerleader at Florida Atlantic University in Boca Raton, Florida. He stated that it was his birthday the night of this incident, and he claimed that he and his friends were drinking and celebrating a few blocks away on the famous Fort Lauderdale "strip" near the corner of Las Olas Boulevard and A1A.

Scott claimed that he'd gotten so drunk that he simply wandered into a home that he *thought* was his friend's, a friend who happened to live close by. This "strip" area, as it turns out, is only a half dozen blocks from the pastor's neighborhood, and the date reflected on Scott's identification for his birthday did actually correspond with the date of the incident.

It seemed that his story about being extremely drunk and wandering into the wrong home — confusing the Thompson home with the home of another friend — was getting more plausible. It sounded even more credible when we understood just how inebriated the young man was at the time of the incident, corroborated by the police officer's observations.

Given the fact that his birthday was, in fact, the same day as the date of the burglary incident, and the fact that the bars in which he was drinking were located in close proximity of the Thompson home, Scott's story was becoming quite credible.

Truth or consequences

Scott swore to us at that table at the rainbow Diner that he was not in the preacher's home for any inappropriate purpose. In an abundance of caution, however, I told Scott that he would need to undergo a polygraph examination at his own expense, to help convince us that he was not in the Thompson home to harm anyone.

He agreed to take the polygraph exam to help prove that he was telling the truth. We explained to him that a polygraph examination was not always determinative of the truth, but that his willingness to undergo such an examination was certainly going to help his cause, especially if he passed the exam.

As it turned out, Scott passed the exam. The polygraph charts showed no deception whatsoever, indicating that he was being truthful. Frank Carbone, the past president of the Florida Polygraph Association, was the polygraphist. He was convinced that Scott was telling the truth in *not* knowing why he was in the home, that he intended no harm to Jennifer, or the pastor, or Cynthia, or anybody else within the home. Scott was required to pay for the polygraph examination from his own funds, and it cost him $500.

He also knew that we were going to compare his fingerprints with the latent fingerprints left at several other crime scenes in the neighborhood. There were a couple of rapes that had occurred within seven or eight blocks of the Thompson home over the last several months before this incident.

He quickly agreed to this fingerprint comparison, apparently not realizing that we didn't need his agreement at all to conduct the print comparison. We reached out to Detective Sonia Friedman of the Sex Crimes Unit to conduct the fingerprint comparison. Scott's prints did not match with any of those prints from those earlier crime scenes, and when we factored into the equation the polygraph results and all the other circumstances in this case, we determined he was telling the truth.

"The burglar and the preacher have the same lawyer?"

It was at this point that the pastor agreed that I could now represent Scott. I then secured a waiver of the obvious conflict of interest in my representing Scott after first representing the pastor. Both men signed the express waivers of the otherwise applicable conflict of interest, and the prosecutor and I agreed to resolve the case by way of a plea disposition.

The assigned prosecutor, Sharon Mullane, helped me to resolve this case at the "case filing level," agreeing *not* to file the felony burglary charge; instead, she was deferential to the victims and did the right thing by filing a misdemeanor trespass charge. This reduced charge, made possible in large measure by the request of Pastor Thompson and his wife, was a *huge* victory for Scott.

It never gets more benevolent than this, with the *victim* actually *requesting* the felony burglary charge be reduced to a misdemeanor trespass! We agreed that there would be certain *conditions* attached to that decision to file the trespass charge; those conditions included a period of probation, both secular and faith-based counseling, no drugs or alcohol, random urinalysis, and 12-step meetings.

The sun was now going down and the air was cooling down while I still lay there on the lawn, but my memory of this case was only warming up.

Pastor and Cynthia Thompson, as I recalled, threw in a few additional special conditions which were otherwise arguably unenforceable, including the condition that Scott would come to First Baptist Church and sit under the preaching of the word for four consecutive Sundays, with the understanding that he was on his own after that.

He could continue there, or go somewhere else, or

discontinue going to church. But in the meantime, they wanted to make sure he was exposed to a Bible-believing church and that he had ample opportunity to hear the gospel message.

Scott brought his aunt with him, a Catholic nun, on those four occasions when he attended First Baptist Church. His aunt, I recall, made a special point of letting us know that she really enjoyed the services.

Then there was the gift I gave him. I almost forgot that I had given him the special gift of a personalized and engraved leather-bound Bible (the same type of "Student Bible" my wife had given me when we married), along with a personalized letter including all of my favorite Scriptures of encouragement. After *all* of this, he must have felt that we were total nut jobs, or that indeed, he had a legion of angels watching over him!

Ever find yourself in the middle of a miracle?

Can you imagine being Scott for a moment in this story? He gets drunk and finds himself in a stranger's home, and the next thing he knows, he's being surrounded by police officers who are cursing at him and threatening to blow his head off. And if that were not surprising enough, the next thing he knows, he's being visited by a criminal defense attorney and his private investigator. He's then invited down the street to a popular diner to meet with the unknown lawyer and the investigator, only to then meet the victim of the burglary along with the lawyer. He finds out that the victim is a pastor; and then the pastor and the lawyer talk to him about God. They ask him whether or not he has a personal and committed relationship with Jesus Christ, and before he knows it, he agrees to come to church.

He is then given a Bible with his name on it, along with dozens of relevant Scriptures. If this were not surprising enough, he learns that the preacher/burglary victim and the criminal defense attorney, together with the prosecutor, agree to dismiss the burglary charge and place him on a period of probation on a reduced misdemeanor charge of trespass, essentially making his troubles go away!

Lying there on the grass at TRC, I asked my imaginary audience, "What would you think if you were Scott in this story? Would you think that you were surrounded by nutcases? Or could it be that you walked into the middle of a miracle? Could your Heavenly Father have been looking out for you? Was He speaking to you through your circumstances? Was He guiding you to get the help you need? Was He giving you a second chance?

"These things actually happened to Scott. If they had happened to you, wouldn't you believe that God's angels were doing some heavy lifting in helping you, and that God was really working in your life, surrounding you with people of faith?"

My imaginary jury was nodding with me in agreement as the sun ducked down and the wind blew the tree branches above me.

All the players in Scott's case were blessed by the grace, mercy and forgiveness demonstrated by Pastor Larry and Cynthia Thompson.

And here it was that I was *still* benefiting from this example a year later as I lay on the grass outside of Atlanta, thinking of my own miracle and thanking the awesome God of second chances.

Chapter 25

Corporate Espionage

"One more week and I'm outa Atlanta and back with my family!" I shouted with joy to myself.

As I contemplated the sweetness of that thought, I inexplicably remembered the Fishler* family and the shock they experienced upon the arrest of their young son. As parents, they appeared to have done everything right!

Fear started to rear its ugly head again, only this time I knew exactly where it was coming from. It was the enemy, trying to steal my joy, wanting me to believe that the same things may happen to me and my family, with my children now at greater risk because of my past.

"Get lost, you loser," I told that spirit of fear and discouragement. My strength was in Christ, and I immediately tapped into Him and prayed for my kids and their future. It was then that I reflected back on Andy Fishler's true story, and how *again* the God of second chances had come through with His redemptive plan for yet another young man!

Sitting back in a chair with a cup of coffee in hand, I relived the Andy Fishler case as though it were just last week. I could almost hear the FBI Agents during their surveillance of young Andy:

...

"You gotta be joking," said the older agent to his partner. "He's not much more than a kid."

"Tell me about it, I got a kid about his age."

"What in the world is this kid gonna do with 10 grand?"

"Well, 10 won't take you too far today, especially when it ain't yours, when you didn't earn it. Besides, he thinks it's Office Depot's dough, not the Bureau's."

Andrew Fishler's case involved strippers, the FBI,

* *This family's name was changed to protect their privacy.*

corporate espionage, and a young man in very big trouble. He worked as a graphic designer for Office Depot; and now he was caught in a FBI sting operation, essentially for spying on Office Depot and attempting to sell his insider information.

"I don't think he's working this alone…do you? You figure he's just a mule for the real players?"

"I don't know, but I hope he doesn't go far, cause we're low on gas."

"No way! I got the coffee. You were supposed to gas up, Sherlock."

"We're supposed to let the money walk, not get away."

"There he goes, don't lose him, or we'll look like village idiots."

"I'm not losing him, not to worry, I haven't lost one yet."

"There he is; let's keep him closer, will ya? I don't wanna be back on the desk any time soon."

"I got him, chill out."

"Check this out, he's pulling into that strip joint!"

"Oh, well, duty calls. We're gonna have to go in too."

"Yeah, tough duty. The commander is not gonna believe this, no way."

"So much for big time corporate espionage, huh?"

After watching the kid in action for some time, one of the agents observed, "Hey, he' spending the Bureau's dough a lot faster than we are. Check him out; and the way those chicks are flocking to him, he's gotta be tipping 'em big time. Can you believe this kid's throwing all the money away on strippers?"

…

Fishler, who later became my client, was indicted by federal Grand Juries in two states, Massachusetts and Ohio, in March of 2000. It was just a year before I came to TRC. His indictments alleged that he had committed a total of 21 federal counts of wire fraud and seven counts of mail fraud.

Specifically, he was indicted out of Boston and again out of Cleveland, for attempting to sell Office Depot's internal corporate pricing information, to competitors OfficeMax and Staples.

Fishler worked for Office Depot, the victim, allowing him access to privileged pricing information — Office Depot's intellectual property. He committed separate counts of "wire fraud" every time he used a phone line to communicate by email with his employer's competitors.

Little did he know, but the executives at OfficeMax and Staples did the right thing and went straight to the FBI, instead of taking the bait. In fact, it was the FBI that sent him the money.

The FBI then secured a wiretap order to trace and then monitor all of Fishler's email activity. The emails originated from behind all sorts of "firewalls" connected to a fictitious name and Hotmail account set up on the Hawaiian Island of Maui. He was creative, as well as dishonest.

The Bureau sent Fishler the money, believing that they had stumbled onto some sort of huge, and perhaps international, corporate espionage case. They would have to send and then "follow the money," if they ever hoped to see how big this thing was, how many corporate players, etc.

They thought it might even lead them to organized crime. Instead, it led them to a kid out of high school only a few years and to South Florida strip joints. The federal agents and federal prosecutors could hardly believe it — Fishler blew the FBI's money on strippers.

The Fishler family hired me soon after Andy's indictments. Based on what I knew about them, I thought of them as a strong faith-filled family. Now, their son, who had lived a seemingly exemplary life for over 20 years, was looking at a prison sentence for just as long.

This court case became a very complicated one because all

companies involved were headquartered in different states. Federal criminal charges were filed (and fought) in three different cities: Fort Lauderdale, Boston, and Cleveland. I traveled a lot that year in order to properly defend my client.

Defending a federal client in two states simultaneously can be quite challenging, to say the least, especially when you are a one-man show like me. This was a highly visible case, because of the involved big corporations, and the intrigue of corporate espionage.

This defense would require travel to Boston, where Staples is headquartered, and to Cleveland, the corporate headquarters for OfficeMax.

Fortunately, I was used to handling complicated cases which required extensive travel. The Sean Maroney defense — "Hemingway Bandit" bank robbery cases from a few years back — served as an excellent confidence-builder, reminding me that I'd done this kind of good work before and had done it effectively. That kind of brazen and borderline-reckless confidence is necessary, I found, in order to pull off the unthinkable.

I worked out a multi-jurisdictional, concurrent deal with the U.S. attorney's offices in Cleveland and Boston. In this situation, it seemed that the outcome of the case was dependent partly upon developing a rapport with the prosecutors.

The defense of mitigation ("you got me, please help me") would need to be first sold to the involved FBI agents, and then to the prosecutors, by first selling *myself* as a family man of faith. They needed to view me as someone who simply wanted to help a young man who was in over his head, a young man with no criminal history who obviously needed help.

Two prosecutors in distant cities in two states agreed that this was a young man crying out for help. He was diagnosed as having a "generalized anxiety disorder," an affliction that, according to one doctor at TRC, I may have coincidentally shared.

The *Sun-Sentinel* quoted me as saying: "[My client] recognized that he had no chance of getting away with this. He is willing to accept responsibility for his actions and recognizes that there are consequences for bad choices." Sounds like I was talking about myself.

The involved prosecutors were asked to embrace truths that they normally don't champion in court: mercy, redemption, and second chances. Those were the products I was selling. This may have been my own desperate cry for help, as I was finding out in Atlanta. If you believe in the product, you'll be successful in selling it, I'm told.

Referring to young Andy, I asked each federal prosecutor, "Give him a second chance, please, given his youth and lack of any prior criminal history. This young man needs help. He is wrestling with some real issues of repressed sexuality, a generalized anxiety disorder, and a real struggle now in his faith. Please help me, to help him."

In the end, Fishler never spent a day in jail.

"The angels must've been working overtime in the lives of everybody connected with Andy's case," I thought to myself.

The outcome of the case was amazing. After publicly admitting that he had been scheming to get money to frequent strip bars, Andy Fishler received a very cushy sentence of only three years of probation.

Thank God that He blessed Andy with a second chance. It was important to me that Andy got that second chance. It was also important to me that I was privileged to be a part of God's redemptive plan for Andy's life. He was a good person who just made some stupid mistakes, not unlike me.

Young Andrew Fishler graduated from the same private Christian school attended even today by one of my own children. His parents are the quintessentially nice, sweet spirited and wonderful parents that countless children on this planet could only dream about.

And yet, all the best parenting and all that private Christian education couldn't keep him from committing federal felonies; and to be sure, none of it could keep him out of the strip joints.

Within a week I'd be leaving the treatment center. It dawned on me that I would need to remember this fact. Like most parents today, I expect too much from our schools. In our frenetic and harried pace today to "be all that we can be," we become "human doings," instead of "human beings," just as they taught us at TRC.

The church pastors do a good job of reminding us that we too often "outsource" our responsibilities as parents and lean on the schools to be our "subcontractors," to do a lot of our heavy lifting as surrogate parents.

It was never the school's job to be our kids' teachers of Biblical values, morality, and life's lessons and truths. It has always been *our* job, as God's selected parents for our children, to instruct them on the kind of thought life that they should entertain, and to remind them of the very real consequences in this life for the choices that we make.

The truth is, even if we do all of this and do it well — just as the Fishler parents did — still our kids are ultimately the *only* ones responsible for their own poor choices. We are only responsible for doing the next right thing; we are not responsible for the result.

I got to thinking: Too many people today are playing the blame game; and, just as wrong, too many parents today are beating themselves up over the poor choices made by their kids — even when the kids are *my* age! I imagine my own parents have occasionally wondered about *themselves,* whenever we adult kids made poor choices — like my own that eventually led me to Atlanta.

All we can do is *all* we can do, while praying all the while that our kids will remember *who* they are, and better yet, *whose* they are. That's where *we* really come in, to teach them *whose* they are. Our best hope is that our children will always be cognizant of a greater audience to whatever they do, remembering that our Heavenly Father is omnipresent and omniscient, always there and always aware, with love.

Our kids can blow us off and ignore the instructions we've given them — just as I must've done with my own parents. But one thing is certain: There's no blowing off the One who made them and died for them, the One who is *always* there with them, even when we're not — the One who promised them repeatedly that He will *never* leave them nor forsake them.

Chapter 26

Preacher Teacher

Before leaving Atlanta, I just had to say good-bye to Pastor
Jerome Dukes. So, I asked Tommy and Eddie — another
friend who was a famous WWF wrestler — to go with me to
church and to the mall afterwards. They'd already committed
to Sanjay that he'd be their "third" guy — to satisfy the whole
"traveling in threes" requirement — getting him all excited
about checking out the women at the Lenox Mall that
afternoon. The three of them had even planned to attend the
obligatory "outside meeting" in one of the rooms in Buckhead
near the mall after dinner. Sanjay was in the equation, then, no
matter what, so compromise was inevitable.

We stopped by the church that final Sunday as Pastor
Dukes was already preaching. The fact that he was already
preaching meant we had timed it perfectly to miss the worship
part of the service. That was the only way I could get my TRC
buddies to come along with me. They had let me know earlier
that morning how they felt.

"There's no way I'm sitting through all that hollering again.
The singing went on forever and ever, and with all those
people raising their hands in the air and dancing in the pews,
I can't handle that Contini," complained Sanjay.

"But it's not just singing — that's the *worship* part of the
service, where the Holy Spirit can move in your heart and in
your spirit."

"Hey, move this Contini," he offered sarcastically.

"And *you* of all people, Sanjay, need all the help you can
get with that twisted heart and spirit of yours. And hey, I don't
do the hand raising thing either, but that doesn't mean I'm
right and they're not. Maybe they're just more connected in
the Spirit. And all kidding aside, let me tell you, the Holy

Spirit can move all through the room sometimes, and it can get you *really* feeling connected —"

"Hey, I got your connection right here, Contini," he interrupted, grabbing himself this time in a very suggestive way and making the others laugh. You want to play holy roller and sing your brains out and raise your hands up for an hour before he starts preaching, be my guest, but then I ain't going."

"Come on, Sanjay," I tried, but the crowd was with him.

"If you want, we'll get there when the preacher's running his mouth, but that's all I can handle before the mall," he continued.

I gave it my best with Sanjay for a while longer, but he already had the others convinced that we'd go only if they didn't have to sit through all the singing. I cut the best deal I could, figuring it was better than nothing. I hated to compromise, but I was learning the hard way that I'd better get skilled at compromise, if I wanted to get along with others.

…

"Your *feelings* need to flow from your *actions*, and not your *actions* from your *feelings*! Worldly feelings and emotions lead to worldly decisions and actions, amen! Don't let your emotions and feelings control your thoughts and actions. Let His *Word* control your thoughts and actions, can I get a witness!"

Pastor Dukes was on a roll now. The amen's were echoing in rhythm with the head nodding. Just then, I was overcome by the realization that I was really going to miss this church, this preacher, and these sweet people.

"Look at the word, right here in 1 Corinthians 15:33-34. Read along with me, Church, right now, go: "Do not be misled: Bad company corrupts good character. Come back to your senses as you ought, and stop sinning."

"Family, you cannot *think* your way into right *acting*; you have to *act* your way into right *thinking*! Your feelings and emotions will get you in trouble every time! Believers, it's a constant struggle between *our* will versus *God's* will for our lives; we should pray we *lose*, for if we *lose*, we *win*! That's the strange paradox; if *our* will loses to *God's* will for our life, we really *win*!"

It was obvious that the congregation was enjoying the message. Even Tommy and Eddie were into it.

I recall thinking to myself, "Thank you, God, that you gave me a couple of nice guys at TRC who I *didn't* have to *pay* to come to church with me."

Eddie and Tommy looked at me approvingly, and then to each other in obvious agreement, even nodding their heads as the preacher pressed on. Then I stole a look at Sanjay and almost busted a gut.

Poor Sanjay, he looked like he was hating life. I made a mental note to myself to get alone with him later and do my best to share my faith with him. "You've got to get alone with him, John," I remember repeating to myself, "since he loves to play to an audience!"

...

"An intelligent man will *not* invest in the corruptible, in a dying concern, the flesh; instead, he owes a debt to the *Spirit*, and invests *there*, in what is *not* going to perish, in his eternity! Come on, talk to me now!

"Men, listen to me — you ladies too — can I get a witness! If I see what I ain't supposed to see, and I hear what I ain't supposed to hear, and I say what I ain't supposed to say, I'm eventually gonna do what I ain't supposed to do! The devil — come on, talk to me now! — the devil, or sin, takes you further than you ever wanted to go, he keeps you longer than you wanted to stay, and you pay more than you ever wanted to pay!"

"Amen!"…"Oh, Lordie!"…"Preach it, Pastor!" several shouted around us.

...

We said our good-byes when the service wrapped up. And we got hugs from *everyone* around us, as the choir was singing and rocking to the beat of the music. Even Sanjay was hugging people, and I remember smiling big and thanking God for that; but then I noticed he was engaging in a highly selective hugging campaign of sorts.

He was shaking hands with the older and bigger women, and only hugging the younger, very attractive women, eyeballing Tommy with that stupid grin of his as he was doing it. "He's going to need a lot more time and a lot more talking to," I recall telling myself.

Then I locked eyes with Pastor Dukes before we made a beeline for one another. He hugged me as big as life, like he was squeezing the sin out of me!

"I love you, Preacher. God used you in my life."

"I love you too, John. Now, let us know when you come back. We'll send you the tapes, and you keep in touch with us, you hear?"

...

We weren't in that church parking lot for more than a couple seconds before Sanjay was goofing on everyone and mocking some of what he had heard and experienced. But then thankfully my mall-doll buddy, Tommy, deflected him quite artfully by enthusiastically suggesting, "You guys up for the Lenox Mall?"

"Sure," I replied, squinting through the hot Georgia sun, "why not, something different for a change. If we're gonna plummet from this spiritual high, we might as well land on all the other mannequins at the mall."

Eddie, normally very quiet and quite expressionless, was smiling big as I added, "But then Eddie and I will need a pick-me-up, Tommy — a little caffeine —"

"What about me?" protested Sanjay, acting a bit hurt and left out.

"Of course you too, Sanjay — especially now that you've hopefully acknowledged all your sins. You must be tired and need a pick-me-up, after all that heavy lifting in confessing all your sins back there. Come to think of it, you probably needed a lot more time to dump your sin bucket," I teased.

"Very funny, Contini," is all he muttered, figuring he abused me enough that morning. Tommy and Eddie were laughing again, but thankfully so was Sanjay. He and I then smiled at each other as a sign of agreeing to let it go for now. And I picked right back up where I was in mid-sentence, before Sanjay interrupted me.

"— and then of course, the world famous meatloaf at the Buckhead Diner." I added, "What do you say?"

Tommy nodded his silent consent as he drove, and then when it got way *too* quiet again, he broke us all up with his sigh and refrain, "Malling and meatloaf — it doesn't get any better than that."

Chapter 27

The Hemingway Bandit

The next day, back at TRC, Tom Porter and I met for another session. After the usual pleasantries, Tom inquired about a legal case I'd mentioned before. "So this guy that your cop friend referred to you — he was what you called a serial bank robber?"

"His name is Sean Maroney; but the Massachusetts authorities called him the "Hemingway Bandit," because his notes to the bank tellers were far too long. He was too verbose, reminiscent of the famous author. He'd write, 'This is a robbery. I have a gun. Put the money in the bag. No exploding die packs, only small bills: 20s, 50s...' and then his notes would continue on and on."

"Whatever happened to him — this guy, Maroney? You said your police friend helped him out?" Porter asked, even more curious now.

"Oh, it's a great story. Are you sure you have the time?" I asked.

"Yeah, for that, sure. It sounds more interesting than sitting here listening to you tell me how you've forgiven someone you really haven't forgiven, or reading through your discharge papers," Porter quipped, smiling ear to ear.

"You're funny, Tom. But you're right — it's definitely more interesting than whether I forgive or don't forgive some other guy, or reading my otherwise colorful discharge papers."

"Tell me then," he insisted.

"Sean Maroney robbed three banks in Worcester County, Massachusetts — all three in the city of Worcester. He robbed another bank in Middlesex County — in Cambridge. There was one in Essex County — in Lynn. And then there was the one in Suffolk County — in Boston, the federal case, among a few others. All in all, he robbed 11 banks throughout the Commonwealth of Massachusetts, before absconding from his federal parole and fleeing to Florida, where he robbed the Jefferson Bank in Hollywood."

Porter was wide-eyed and almost laughing at how brazen this kid, Maroney, was.

"Poor Jefferson," I added, getting off the subject for a moment. "He'd be rolling over in his grave if he knew that a bank had been named after him. After all, it was Jefferson who said, 'Banks are more dangerous to our liberties than standing armies.'"

"Jefferson said that? I knew I liked Jefferson," Porter interrupted.

"It was the bank in Florida that led to my representation of Maroney. My cop friend, Detective Richy Allen, was the Hollywood police sergeant involved in processing Maroney after his arrest; and coincidentally, Allen was from Maroney's neighborhood in South Boston. They spoke with identical accents that each of them immediately recognized. Then again, of course they'd recognize one of their own; they were from the same Irish neighborhood area dubbed 'Southie.'

"Until Maroney recognized my buddy Detective Allen's accent, he had been a 'John Doe,' refusing to identify himself to the arresting officers. But then upon hearing from one of his own, he asked for the detective's help. 'Can you do anything to help me, get me a good lawyer, a deal to something I can live with?' Sean asked my detective friend with the 'Southie' accent. The two of them got along so famously that they even compared tattoos, knowing from childhood gang stuff that they'd each have the same tattoo on their hips, and they did.

"Detective Allen gave him my name and then did even one better; he actually called me himself, asking me to visit Maroney in jail. He recommended me to Maroney's parents and went so far as to lobby a bit on his behalf with the assigned prosecutor in Broward."

Porter reflected on what he'd just heard.

"So your cop buddy did *him* a favor by setting him up with a good lawyer, and he did that because the guy confessed to him. And of course he'd have a special affinity for a kid from the old neighborhood back home. And he did *you* a favor by giving you a case that you would not have otherwise gotten, right?"

Porter was right so far, as usual.

"True, the Hemingway Bandit case was my golden opportunity to work as a lawyer in my home state of Massachusetts, so in that sense he *did* do me a favor. But then I think he was *really* doing the favor for Sean Maroney, not me — hooking him up with a Boston lawyer, knowing like he did that I was also licensed as a lawyer in Massachusetts."

"Maybe *both* of you, did you ever think of that?" Porter added.

"Well, it *was* a professional homecoming of sorts, regardless of who he did it for, a real big-time-lawyer experience back home that I had not previously experienced. I got to travel all over my home state defending Maroney.

"What was this bank robber kid like?"

"Maroney was a very handsome young man, and he had an interesting way he'd stake out banks. He was a real lady's man and often went on dates with attractive young women. Prior to a robbery, he took his dates to his targeted banks, and he'd park his car in front of the bank building. Some women would ask why they were there, and he'd tell 'em he was admiring the architecture. Can't you just picture it, Tom?

"'What are we doing here?' a date might ask him.

"'Oh, I'm just admiring the architecture. Some of these banks are built so beautifully, don't you think?'

"'Sure, I guess, but what do you want to do tonight? I'm hungry. Can we go out to dinner now?'

"Maroney wouldn't be thinking about what the young

woman might prefer to do on a date. All he'd be thinking about was how he was going to rob that bank. Would it be as easy as the others? How was he going to get out of there? Where should he direct his taxi driver to let him out? Where does he want the cabbie to wait? Around which corner? Where's he going to get his junk, his next fix?

"He was a junkie?" Porter asked, seemingly surprised.

"Oh yeah, Maroney's worst problem was that he was a heroin junkie. His second problem was that he had a propensity to rob banks in order to get the money for the junk. Things got worse for him when he got one of these women pregnant, and when she found out about all the other women and all the banks he'd been robbing, she made it her business to testify against him.

"Hell hath no fury like a woman scorned," Porter quipped again, reminding me of that old saying.

"True," I agreed. "And Sean Maroney had already been convicted for robbing one bank, netting himself a fairly benevolent two-year federal prison sentence from U.S. District Court Judge Mazzone."

"That's all he got?" asked Porter, as surprised as I was over what appeared to be a very lenient sentence for the young man.

"Yes, but Judge Mazzone kept jurisdiction over Maroney, because he'd be on parole once he was released from prison. And most people knew they'd never want to have to reappear in front of Mazzone on a violation of their federal parole. This Judge didn't play. Judge Mazzone was a renowned federal judge in Massachusetts and a longtime friend of the Kennedy family. He played football with Robert Kennedy at Harvard, and he was the one who officiated the marriage ceremony for Teddy Kennedy. Mazzone was no ordinary federal judge. He helped to write the now infamous U.S. Sentencing Guidelines while he was on the United States Sentencing Commission. Bottom line: He knew he could slam Maroney any time he wanted if the kid screwed up on his federal parole.

"It was upon his release from prison and before the ink even dried on his parole papers, that Sean robbed a *dozen* other banks all over the Commonwealth, before absconding from Massachusetts; and then as a fugitive, he landed in South Florida and robbed the Jefferson Bank in Hollywood, Florida."

"What the —" Porter started to talk but could then only laugh at the thought of this young man robbing banks all over Massachusetts after getting such a break before.

"Coincidentally, the Jefferson Bank was *my* own bank, where I kept my money!" I added to this funny and ironic visual.

"When I heard it had been robbed, I had no way of knowing that I would defend the bank robber."

"This young man must have gotten slammed by that famous federal judge when he got caught again, right? I mean, you're a good lawyer, I'm sure, but sometimes a dozen bank robberies will just be way too much, right?"

Porter saw the big picture way ahead of me, as I never gave the expected result much thought when I took the case.

"Oh, the story of what ultimately happened to him by this judge is a story in itself!" I emphasized, only peaking Porter's interest even more. His eyes widened once again.

"I worked on the Hemmingway Bandit case for two years. I had to build a rapport with the involved prosecutors in every affected county in Massachusetts. The development and management of relationships in the legal world is just as important as it is in any other world; I set out to get these folks to know and trust me, probably like you guys do with us here at TRC. And the same thing was absolutely necessary before any of the involved prosecutors — they call 'em 'assistant district attorneys' up there — would start making decent deals with me.

"Sean Maroney was looking at several decades in jail if his sentences were stacked consecutively. I asked each prosecutor — again, only after becoming friendly with them — for *concurrent* or simultaneously-running sentences. My personal and informal meetings with them were critically important."

"I bet they were," replied Tom, picturing the whole scenario.

"Suffice it to say, I just knew in my spirit that this would be necessary. Maybe a few of the sharper defense lawyers from out of town had done this with me back when I was a prosecutor, I don't recall. The crucial question was whether or not these particular prosecutors would go along with *concurrent* sentencing — meaning that Maroney's sentence for robbing *their* particular county's bank, could run simultaneously with the sentences that he would receive in other counties.

"This question about concurrent sentencing had to be asked of each of them in *person*, only after our rapport or relationship had been established — once we got to laughing about whatever we might have had in common — so I was driving all over the Commonwealth of Massachusetts that week, having a good time at night by the way — imbibing whatever I wanted, whenever I wanted.

"Now, don't be romancing that drink again," Porter warned.

"I won't," I replied, lamenting the thought that I'd not be doing that again.

"Getting back to this case ... Where was I? Oh yeah, the question had to be asked as almost an afterthought — like the way the TV detective Colombo would often stop and ask a belated question as he was leaving a meeting. The typical answer from these prosecutors was, 'It doesn't matter to me, what do I care?'

"In our first big hearing out in Worcester County, the prosecutor with Commonwealth of Massachusetts recommended 18 to 20 years as the prison sentence for Maroney's Worcester County bank robberies. He had robbed three banks in the City of Worcester, causing some real panic in the city. It was in this city, the one actually *most* affected, that he earned his nickname in the media, the 'Hemingway Bandit.'

"I ran my mouth for what seemed like a half hour with all kinds of passion, and I could tell the Judge was receptive and really listening. It was obvious that I had the clerk and the probation officer going with me, nodding their heads in approval, which only encouraged me to continue. Getting the Court's personnel to go with you is sometimes half the battle; because if *they* like you, *and* your guy, and whatever it is you're arguing, they can be quite influential on the judge. Judges can sense what their own people would prefer to see happen, just by their looks and the little nonverbal cues they tend to unwittingly telegraph to one another.

"We had earlier tried to negotiate an agreement with the Assistant D.A. for anything less than 12 to 20, but they wouldn't budge from 12. These were the only prosecutors in the Commonwealth who refused to get on the same page with me before the scheduled hearings. And that turned out to be good news, in retrospect, because we ended up doing *better* with the judge.

"Thankfully, I prevailed upon the involved Worcester County judge, Judge Traures, to sentence Maroney to only eight years, of which he'd serve only four and a half! Judge Traures went far below the guidelines, which is almost never done.

"Maroney's parents and then current fiancé started crying and hugging me, and then hugging each other. Needless to say, I was on a high after that moment. And that sentence ended up being a barometer of sorts — or the benchmark of appropriate sentencing for the other involved prosecutors and judges, when considering what ought to happen on all the other bank robberies. That low ball sentence helped to resolve the other bank robbery cases throughout the Commonwealth, as I was then able to leverage the Worcester County sentence to support my already established rapport with each individual Assistant District Attorney."

"Wow!" is all Porter would say, jaw dropping to emphasize his shock over these sentencing results.

"When each and every plea deal was cemented and each of the concurrent sentences were pronounced, it was obvious to everyone that Maroney would be out of prison and back home in four years *at a theater near you* — not bad for robbing over a dozen banks!"

Porter was just shaking his head in disbelief, working up a half smile and a look that made me think he was sort of proud of his young student — a look like my father would give me.

Chapter 28

Legal Logistics

Tom Porter was seemingly amazed by the story about the Hemingway Bandit case, especially by the light sentence Sean Maroney received.. His amazement and facial expressions only encouraged me to give him more on the behind the scenes logistics of how we got it all done.

"And check this out, Tom. The challenges we faced in the court cases themselves, almost pale in comparison to the challenges inherent in transporting Maroney from one courthouse to another. The logistics involved in coordinating all the involved sheriffs' transport deputies, county by county, and all the behind-the-scenes orchestration in this administrative prison transport quagmire, became a *huge* part of this case, my *biggest* challenge.

"This was a multi-county, multi-jurisdictional, state and federal *puzzle*, and if it weren't put together in just the right way, not only would it not work; it would be one *ugly* puzzle picture for Sean and the entire Maroney family.

"Wow," is all Porter said.

"Sean, the prisoner, had to be transported from jail to jail, county to county, with no margin of error for transport or logistics delays; otherwise, he would be missing for court in that next county's scheduled sentencing. And if we missed even *one*, then that would throw off *everything*, running the risk that we'd mess it up in a dominos kind of fashion, and miss out on *all* the rest of the concurrent sentencing we had worked out! Had that happened, then at least one of these bank robbery cases would *still* be outstanding, subjecting Maroney to probable *consecutive* sentencing — meaning the next sentence would not run or begin until *after* his concurrent sentencing on all the other bank robbery cases! That would mean several additional years in prison for Sean, at a minimum.

"Unbelievable," Porter added. "These are things you'd never think about as a layman."

"To guard against this probability, I schmoozed all the right prison transport guys and the administrative deputies for each and every respective county. These so-called 'little people' are the ones who really make the big system run, one way or another.

"And I received help from a most unusual source. Judge Mazzone *himself* had called the Salem Superior Court judge, the prison officials at MCI-Cedar Junction (Walpole), and then the U.S. Marshal's Office, to actually help me with one major problem that reared its ugly head. Typical of government apathy and turf issues, two different governments — the feds and the Commonwealth of Massachusetts — refused to budge or cooperate with one another in their petty little transport contest.

"They were at an impasse over *whose* responsibility it was to get Sean Maroney over to Essex County, the City of Lynn, from Judge Mazzone's federal courtroom."

"You're serious?" Porter asked, looking just as disapprovingly as Mazzone did when he found out about the beef.

"Serious as a heart attack, I couldn't make any of this up. The Commonwealth and their sheriffs' transport deputies were saying that it was the federal government's responsibility to transport the *federal* inmate out of the *federal* hearing and *federal* courthouse, regardless of the next appointed destination — even if that next location was a *Commonwealth* hearing. "Meanwhile, the feds — or the deputy U.S. marshals — were saying that it was the *Commonwealth's* responsibility to come and pick up their *Commonwealth* prisoner, if they wanted him transported to another *Commonwealth* courthouse for yet another *Commonwealth* bank robbery case. We were all at a standstill, as the wheels of justice figuratively ground to a halt."

"What did that federal judge do to help you?" Porter was caught up in the story, as was I again. It was all coming back to me and reliving it was kind of fun, getting me ready to go back to doing my lawyer thing in Fort Lauderdale.

"Can you believe it, Tom, a *federal* judge — appointed by the President of the United States for *life*, calling records personnel at the prison and other transport personnel? He took it upon himself to proactively help orchestrate Maroney's transport to a state proceeding in a different city, knowing I had a flight to catch at the end of the day. It was incredible!

"The court personnel, two clerks, the probation officer, the prosecutor, and the deputies were all looking at each other and at *me*, as amazed as I was, at his Honor's personal help. He obviously took some liking to me, and he let us all know how impressed he was, by the way.

"Thanks to Judge Mazzone, we secured immediate transportation for prisoner Sean. Then we were off to secure yet another victory, this time on the Essex County bank robbery. The result: the sentence would be concurrent with the Worcester County sentence, with credit for 175 days served! This result was, in effect, a *zero* sentence on each additional bank robbery case!"

"That's incredible," is all Porter muttered.

"I know, it *really*, really was. And then to celebrate, Maroney's mother and father took me out for a celebration lunch, and then they helped me drop off my rental car. They took me to the terminal and hugged me like I was family. They were so appreciative, telling me there would be an envelope with something extra waiting for me back in Florida at my office. I never asked them for more money, but they wanted me to know how grateful they were. The money would have been nice, but it couldn't compare with the very huge, public compliment I was paid earlier that day by a big-time federal judge."

"Did they send you more money?" Porter asked, almost as curiously as I asked *myself* at the time.

"No, they never did. But I think that's typical. People say grandiose things like that when they win the lottery or when their lawyer scores 'em a sweet result in court; but when the excitement wears off and they're back to the reality of taking everything for granted, they rarely follow through."

"That's still disappointing after all you did for their son. They should have let the hugs say everything and never said anything about sending more money if they weren't going to follow up and send it. That's an example, John, of the importance of saying what you mean and meaning what you say. It's a basic integrity issue."

"You're right, because I remember now that it did bother me a bit later when I certainly needed the money and remembered them saying this. I remember looking daily in the mail for it, and yet it never came; so you're right, it soured me on the parents a bit. I recall losing some degree of respect for them, especially the father, who initially met me in his military uniform at a café on Hanover Street in the North end, the Little Italy of Boston. He was a former war hero and he was hurting over the plight of his addicted son. I always thought of him as a man of integrity, so you're right Tom; when they didn't mean what they said or say what they meant — or follow through with what they said they were going to do — I lost some respect for them."

"Well, don't forget that. Let that be a lesson to you and to me, to always say what we mean and mean what we say, so others see us as men of integrity and don't lose respect for us," Porter added.

"That's a good word for me, you're right. I won't forget that when I leave here today," I replied, making a mental note to myself to remember this lesson.

"Did you get a chance to thank that federal judge? You said he paid you a huge public compliment. What was that about?" Tom Porter had heard too much to say goodbye before catching the end of the story.

"Oh, yeah, in all my years as a lawyer, it was the greatest compliment I've ever been paid — and to get it so publicly too — in front of a lot of people, mostly court personnel, marshals, the prosecutor, federal probation, the clerk, and his judicial assistant.

"When all was said and done, Judge Mazzone looked over all the paperwork; and he apparently noticed that in all 11 jurisdictions, I had been able to secure concurrent sentencing — basically the same sentence for each and every bank robbery, running simultaneously with one another.

"This federal judge looked up from reviewing all the Commonwealth sentencing orders on his bench and he said, 'Mr. Contini, how did you do this?'

"I hesitated in answering him, as I didn't quite know whether to feign some degree of humility or tell him with specificity how I had actually gotten it done.

"'If I am ever in trouble, I know who I'm going to call,' he then said, before I could say anything.

"'Wow!' I recall thinking to myself. 'That was the greatest compliment I've ever received as a lawyer.'

"He continued, 'We don't get many lawyers up here who do this quality of work.'

"He said that in front of *other* lawyers?" Tom asked, rather shocked, apparently considering the other lawyers' feelings.

"Now, those comments were *not* made in the courtroom in front of my client or his family, or any other defendant or lawyer unconnected with the case. We were only in chambers; but later that morning when he actually sentenced Maroney in open court, he repeated a shorter version of his complimentary remarks in front of *everyone* in the courtroom. The Judge essentially addressed the Maroney sentencing issues twice.

"We had hammered out most of the agreements *first* in his chambers, but the sentencing had to nonetheless be announced officially on the record again in open court, where we had the greater audience. After the actual sentence was pronounced in open court, Judge Mazzone concluded by saying, 'Mr. Contini, someday you'll have to tell me how you did this.'

"And his comments, Tom, I will *never* forget. It never gets bigger than this, as far as a public compliment and validation goes, and from a federal judge no less!"

Chapter 29

Setting the Prisoner Free

Tom Porter had gotten me to dump my whole bucket on the Hemingway Bandit case. Then he nailed it.

"John, after hearing all this, let me tell you. Your cop friend, this Richy fellow — he did you a tremendous service. He gave you this case that you made some money on, I'm sure; but more importantly, look at the experience you've had as a result of getting this case.

"You got to go home and be a lawyer, as you said, all over your home state of Massachusetts. You said you received your biggest compliment in your professional career, one from a famous federal judge whose words still echo in your soul even today. And think about it, John, this Richy fellow was used in the overall scheme of life to allow for all this to happen for you."

Porter summed up the "Hemingway Bandit" case as he shifted his weight forward in his chair. He'd been biding his time while I recounted Maroney's story. But now Porter's slight smile made me think of the way a contented cat toys with a mouse, not to kill it but to play with it. I knew Tom was ready to pounce on the topic of forgiveness again, so I made it easy for him.

"Sometimes even good friends can do you dirty," I said, taking the conversation back to Mike, the "friend" who set me up.

"John, *you're* the one who has to put it behind *you* and leave this place with *no* resentments. And think about it, my friend. This guy — Mike did you a favor, giving you a good reason to come here to TRC. It's irrelevant where his heart may have been at the time. Like most people, he did what he thought was going to be for *his* benefit. He's struggling through this thing we call life like the rest of us. Cut him a break, John, just as others have cut *you* a break.

"You told me yourself, you got a big break with these federal guys after you were here a few months. You were told, 'It's over, you can go back to your life and not worry about the thought of a federal indictment.' You caught a break. Catch this Mike fellow a break. What do you think?" Porter was making sense.

"I think you're right. I'll give him a break. I'll forgive him for real," I replied, only this time meaning it.

"You'll be glad you did, John. You're the one who will really benefit the most from any forgiveness you extend. The prisoner you set free is *you*. Whenever we forgive someone else — who we've kept locked up in resentments and unforgiveness — we experience a new-found freedom. You see, we're the ones incarcerated or shackled by those chains of bitterness and resentment. So, in your case, John, when you truly forgive, those shackles are broken; and the prisoner you set free is really *you*."

Porter stood up on that parting note to come around his desk for our good-bye hug. I didn't know whether to allow for the tears that were working their way into my eyes, or bust out laughing with the old guy. He was right on the money as usual, and as a fatherly influence in my life during this time, I had developed such affection for him.

"I love you, Tom Porter," is all I said while embracing him good-bye.

"We love you too, John. Now go back home and apply these principles in your daily affairs. That's how you thank me and the rest of us here, OK."

Departing Atlanta

In the ride back to the airport in Atlanta, I reflected on my months at TRC and the close relationships I had formed while there. I could never forget Tom Porter or Dr. Doug Talbott. And I also found myself processing the whole forgiveness issue once again. My own thoughts reminded me that it's not really forgiveness if we're still hanging onto resentments over something in the past, resentments toward someone we believe has wronged us.

The Holy Spirit had convicted me as Porter spoke, and then again as I reflected on my own apparent unforgiveness of Mike. It was true that I had still felt resentment toward my old client and friend; and therefore, I must *not* have really forgiven him, *"from my heart,"* as we're commanded to do in Matthew 18:35.

And if I had continued hanging onto this resentment, it would have been equally true that *I* would *not* be forgiven for the things *I've* done in this world. On this exact issue, Christ told us in Matthew 6:14-15, "For if you forgive men when they sin against you, your Heavenly Father will also forgive you. But if you do not forgive men their sins, your Father will not forgive your sins."

Then as the van rounded the corner to the entrance to the Atlanta airport, Dr. Doug Talbott's words came back to me: "Anger is like acid; it destroys the container in which it is stored as much as the object on which it is poured."

"That old guy is still in my head," I remember saying to myself. Unloading my stuff from the van only hastened my thoughts. Jesus' parable of the unmerciful servant popped into my head. Christ had explained that the King forgave his servant/debtor — the servant who had an inability to repay a huge debt owed to the King.

His point was that *we* are that debtor, that *we* cannot repay that huge "sin debt" we owe. And in that parable, just as quickly as the servant-debtor was forgiven, he himself showed no forgiveness toward his own debtor — even though he was owed a much smaller amount — throwing his own debtor into jail. The King, representing our Heavenly Father in the parable, then "turned him over to the jailers to be tortured, until he should pay back all he owed."

"That would be me," I recall saying to myself as I entered the airport, imagining the Father's disappointment with me for not forgiving the sin debt of another.

Jesus wrapped up the ending to His parable this way: "This is how my Heavenly Father will treat each of you unless you forgive your brother from your heart," referring to the King then throwing the servant into jail to be tortured. (Matthew 18:35).

As I hustled to find my concourse, the message kept reverberating inside my head: We cannot simply pay lip service to forgiveness, while still hanging onto old resentments. I heard the message loud and clear; I understood in my spirit that I needed to finally forgive Mike *from my heart*, or else I wouldn't be forgiven for whatever I've done in life.

After studying the monitors and all the flight and gate information, I joined the river of humanity, making my way to the up escalator to my concourse. My mind was racing faster than the crowd en route to my departure gate.

Keeping in step with the stressed-looking strangers all around me, I struggled with the truth of the fact that forgiveness and consequences are *not* mutually exclusive. There's still the consequence that the relationship will never be the same. A bank robber like Maroney is forgiven, but his consequence of prison still remains. Mike is forgiven, and yet the friendship will never be restored. A spouse can be forgiven for an act of adultery, but the consequence of the loss of trust and intimacy may remain.

Although Sean Maroney was the obvious recipient of an incredible level of heavenly forgiveness and mercy, he still suffered some real earthly consequences for his criminal behavior. I remind my own children of this reality, hopeful that they won't have to learn this life lesson the hard way — Sean's way.

Sean had it all: good parents, a tremendous appearance (a

handsome ladies' man), native intelligence and a gift for communicating — albeit not as gifted as the real Hemingway! My kids are likewise blessed; and for that matter, so was I, but that's the real concern. My blessings were apparently not enough to stop me from making terribly foolish and poor choices along my own self-destructive path in life.

Looking at Sean's life, I think to myself, "There but for the grace of God go I." I never robbed banks, but I've done a lot of other dumb and self-destructive things. It is simply a miracle — or to be more accurate, a series of miracles — that I'm even around to write these heartfelt admonitions to my own kids today.

All of us, like Sean, need to realize that we can use and enjoy all these wonderful gifts given to us by God in the way He intended for us to use them. Or we can use these God-given gifts inappropriately in pursuit of our lustful and selfish desires as we pursue temporary self-gratification. It would almost be comical, if it were not so serious, that we so doggedly pursue self-gratification when we already know in advance the destructive results of self-centered choices.

God willing, my own children will do what Tom Porter and Dr. Doug Talbott and the other counselors taught *me* to do in Atlanta — to stop long enough to do the mental gymnastics and "play the tape forward in our mind" — before following through with the otherwise natural and normal temptation to do inappropriate things.

Approaching my departure gate, I was praying that my children would learn early in life to first "think around the corner," and then to make wise choices, as admonished by Solomon, the writer of Proverbs. His words of wisdom are recorded in Proverbs 3:1-5:

"My son, never forget the things I've taught you. If you want a long and satisfying life, closely follow my instructions. Never forget to be truthful and kind. Hold these virtues tightly. Write them deep within your heart. If you want favor with both God and man, and a reputation for good judgment and common sense, then trust the Lord completely."

At the Gate

The wisdom of Solomon, I thought, caused me to visualize both Tom Porter and Dr. Talbott.

"Wise old men," I mused, as I recalled the way they'd often look at me during our sessions at TRC.

There was a certain look on their face — a kind, caring, and intent look — that I really liked. When they looked at me like that, I felt like they were really listening to me, like I really mattered to them. Then it hit me; it was that agape-kind of love referenced in the Bible! Those two old men, who had been complete strangers just a few months ago, had convinced me that they selflessly cared, that they loved me and of course many others there at TRC, as corny as that sounds. And I had grown to love them too.

It felt odd to sit in the airport with no laptop and no cell phone. Normally, I would use the waiting time and my handheld cell phone to make calls or send wireless e-mails. In fact it felt odd to have *nothing* to do. At TRC, our time was strictly structured and filled with "process groups" and sessions with staff. And before TRC, I was constantly busy, running my law office and doing my lawyer thing. I used every minute of time wherever I was, networking with people, keeping in touch by phone and e-mail — personifying that "human doing" instead of a "human being."

As I sat in the airport, I was feeling insecure and out-of-touch with my own business. I tried telling myself that it was like riding a bike — it would all come back to me — after all, I was the boss and an old pro at all this criminal defense stuff after all this time. At least I kept telling myself this, in hopes that the feelings of insecurity would go away.

Thankfully, I had hired two young attorneys, Marlon Bryan and Ahiza Johnson, to build what I thought would be my own powerful little law firm. At the time, I never imagined that these two younger lawyers would end up running a high-powered legal practice for months without me there.

I was excited about going home and going back to my lawyer gig, but at the same time, I was reluctant. I knew I didn't want things to be the same as before. I'd had lots of time to think things over at TRC; I thought a lot about leaving criminal law and shifting my focus to a distinct area of the law — personal injury and wrongful death.

But then I started feeling very sad.

"Why am I feeling so sad," I wondered, "when I'll soon be with my wife and children again, when life will return to family and friends and the whole lawyer gig again?"

I was drilling myself, trying to figure out where these unexpected emotions were coming from. Then it dawned on me. God was still dealing with me — dealing with my unresolved guilt about defending murder clients who might well have been guilty.

Were these men who ended up acquitted by juries, in fact really guilty? I don't know. They never admitted guilt. And besides, it was the responsibility of the *jury* to determine if they were guilty or not.

I told myself that every client might be an innocent, falsely accused individual, someone who was facing the ultimate penalty for a crime he never committed. But in real life, almost nobody believes that these defendants are falsely accused or innocent. And why didn't I let myself feel for the victims' families? On that issue, I was guilty as sin. But why was this only bothering me now?"

It's true that the murder defendants almost never admit guilt. And there's still the possibility of innocence; but it's equally true that no lawyer can entirely surrender common sense, wisdom, intelligence, morals and a belief system, simply because the lawyer has agreed to advocate a position in court.

Perhaps because of all the "processing" of my issues at TRC, I was feeling everything more acutely. I had peeled away some layers of scar tissue that may have hardened over my desensitized heart. All of a sudden I began feeling more and more guilt over my earlier lack of feelings for the victims and their families. Because of my take-no-prisoners approach to winning in the past, it was likely that guilty clients had walked away without a consequence — even for murder.

Then my tireless ego reared its ugly head yet again, working up yet again the perfect defense. "Wait a minute," the ego said. "You were in the arena, John, and that was no time to get all sentimental. You couldn't allow yourself to think about the victims' families, or to even allow the victim to be humanized at all in your mind, or else you wouldn't have been effective. You're being too hard on yourself."

Then I remembered what Porter taught us: "To 'rationalize' is to tell oneself, 'rational lies.'" I'd been telling myself rational lies for a long time and I was tired of it. I was ready for a change.

I wanted something else to look forward to when I got back, other than some deceiving and unrepentant criminal client possibly wearing a wire on me. That pre-TRC experience of Mike, my friend/contractor/client, betraying me and the feds targeting me, was still quite fresh in my memory; and naturally, I still had trepidations about going back full swing into that world of criminal defense.

That was part of it, but I knew there was more.

Chapter 30

Interrogation of the Soul

I was sleep deprived from cross-examining myself for what seemed like hours the last few restless nights. It was as though the old prosecutor was coming out in me, essentially interrogating my soul, the very core of my being. Suffice it to say, I felt like I was torturing myself into being brutally honest with my *real* self for the very first time.

Then I had an epiphany of sorts, as I decided to quit playing the role of John the big time criminal defense lawyer, or John the Christian lawyer and family man, and all the other roles I had played and perfected. Oh, I'd still be a Christian, and I'd still be a family man and a lawyer; but I wanted to be more real. From now on, I'd just be John the guy hopefully doing the next right thing — whatever that might be, regardless of whatever I was doing.

As I continued this interrogation of my soul, I asked myself, "What do you like best about criminal law?"

"Defending the accused, the downtrodden, the underdog," was my answer to myself. "What did I like least?" The answer came through loud and clear, "Helping some unrepentant, guilty dirt bag walk away a free man!" I recalled that verse from Proverbs 17:15: "Acquitting the guilty and condemning the innocent — the LORD detests them both." I also detested them both.

It was this interrogation that led to the moment of decision. I had long considered a new focus to my legal career, namely, personal injury and wrongful death, or PI for short. As a PI lawyer, I could spend my time fighting for the underdog. I could take on those top dog insurance companies that often took advantage of the little people who naively look to their insurance companies for help and recompense.

I felt relief all of a sudden that I didn't have to wallow in the mud puddle of criminal defense, if I didn't want to anymore. My thoughts were interrupted by the murmur of disapproval that ran through the crowd. While I wasn't paying attention, the waiting room had filled with people preparing to board the plane to Fort Lauderdale. The gate agent announced that we had a brief delay before boarding. The plane was being cleaned and checked out since its late arrival at the gate. That gave me a few minutes to call Marlon, the associate lawyer covering for me back in my office.

The wall phone was greasy and disgusting to the touch, but I refused to let it bother me for more than a second. Holding the receiver away from my ear, I dialed Marlon. The call was picked up immediately.

"Law offices of John Contini and Associates, Marlon Bryan speaking, may I help you?"

"Marlon, John."

After the usual salutations, I started in.

"Marlon, remember I told you that I was thinking about doing personal injury work, wrongful death cases?"

"Yes," he replied.

"Well, now I'm sure. I'm going to get into PI, wrongful death — good civil cases where people are getting hosed by their insurance companies."

"We're really not set up yet to run a personal injury practice," Marlon muttered, sounding concerned.

"I wasn't set up for criminal defense work either, Marlon. When I left the State Attorney's Office and quit being a prosecutor, I started right off doing criminal defense, and though I hadn't done it before, that never stopped me."

"But personal injury work is different," he started to say, before I interrupted him.

"It's all attitude, Marlon. When I had the attitude that I wanted to defend the accused and champion their cause, I worked up a sort of confidence that I was as good as anyone else, and the rest is history."

"I guess you're right," he replied.

"I think so, because the last 15 years of success speaks for itself. And I believe it makes no difference whether it's criminal defense or personal injury. If I believe I can do it and have that sort of confidence — and especially if I believe the little guy is getting screwed by the big wealthy and greedy insurance carrier — I can do it all day long!

"There is just as much unfairness in the world of personal injury and wrongful death — as much if not more than in the criminal defense arena — with insurance carriers sometimes doing the wrong thing by the people and to the people.

"Marlon, these insatiable corporate thieves essentially shake down or extort premiums from the insured clients and ride them like a cheap suit for their monthly premiums — and if the insured is late with the money, they threaten to cancel the policy. The carrier gets all their money from premiums, but when the insured gets hurt, the same insurance carrier refuses to pay the claim — or they certainly try to get away with paying much less than the claim is worth!

"Trust me Marlon, I'm going to have some real fun making these corporate pigs pay what they're supposed to pay to the so called little people. And I can do it all day long without worrying about some dirt bag client wearing a wire on me, or the feds targeting me for something I didn't do."

"What are you going to do with federal clients, especially drug cases and cash?" Marlon asked.

I didn't answer Marlon right away as my mind was spinning with thoughts. I had hired Marlon for all the wrong reasons. He was a younger lawyer I had hired when I *thought* I was big time. I thought I wanted a protégé to teach on occasion. But if I were brutally honest, I wanted a younger lawyer to parade around the courthouse to basically tell all the judges and prosecutors and most importantly my colleagues, "Look at me, I've arrived. I'm doing well enough to pay another lawyer to cover my cases."

Although Marlon was helpful and could do a good job, I learned the hard way that he couldn't really win in the situation I had placed him. Had I been thinking right and using all three parts of my brain, I'd have realized that the clients hired me and not Marlon Bryan or any other associate lawyer I had hired. They wanted *ME* to be there on their behalf and not any of my substitutes — no matter how wonderfully effective they might be as lawyers!

But God, being omniscient, inspired me to hire some help, because He knew in advance that I'd need another lawyer or two to cover for me when I'd run away to treatment.

When I didn't answer his question right away, Marlon switched to a new topic. "Are we still going to be a firm, if you switch to personal injury cases?" Marlon nervously asked.

"Sure, if God continues to provide for us," I replied with strength in my voice. "And we should have plenty of business, because insurance companies, in my opinion, often take advantage of people and pay them only ten cents on the dollar, assuming they don't deny the claim entirely!" I passionately barked into the phone, starting to feel my new calling.

"You hired me a year ago knowing I did personal injury, so I can definitely help in that area better than I can in this criminal area," Marlon added.

"I thought I was hiring you and Ahiza a year ago, believing I was growing this thing, Marlon, but God knew the real reason He had me hire you guys."

"What was that?" Marlon asked, sounding genuinely curious.

"I had another agenda for why I had hired two lawyers to work for me. I was thinking delusionally that I was going to grow a real, big time law firm. But it was all ego — which is spelled, E.G.O., Marlon. I later learned here in the downtown rooms in Atlanta that ego stands for 'easing God out.'

"I was ready to go big time, or so I thought. My heavenly Father was either laughing hysterically, or sad to know in advance what I'd be going through when I fell."

"You know it was the latter, John, as I know how I would feel if my son were about to mess up and I knew it," Marlon replied, finally sounding stronger, thank God.

Marlon and I had a decent working relationship, nice and cordial. We both knew we'd sit down and work things out when I returned. And we both knew we'd be adjusting to big changes. Since my intent was to change the way we'd do business in the future, as a valued associate, he had a right to know then and there.

"Marlon, I've also decided to co-counsel my cases from now on. Working together on criminal cases has worked out well, so I've decided to co-counsel PI cases too. I'll co-counsel these cases with the best PI lawyers in town, board-certified guys like Chuck Prince and Joe Glick. These guys are dug in, and they've even got their own in-house insurance pro, Sal Verini, a former Claims Specialist Manager with Allstate, helping them to administrate the files. They know all the best docs, and they've got paralegals like Rosanne and Joy helping out and working things up. They've tried a million cases, and most importantly, they have that honesty, integrity and work ethic you need to do it right."

"But it takes real money to make money in personal injury and wrongful death work, John, because you have to invest costs in all the files to pay doctors and experts and —"

"Yes, I know grasshopper, and that's why I'm going to use my head this time and co-counsel the cases with the board-certified PI lawyers I mentioned."

Marlon knew that these other lawyers would share or underwrite the up-front expenses in preparing the case, minimizing my costs. So I suspected that Marlon's concern about the firm's finances came from his understandable concern about his own financial future.

"Marlon, I don't know what the future holds for our firm, but I know we'll be in transition for months, at least. And I know I'll need your help, so count on sticking around for at least a year or so. Then we'll assess the situation and go from there, deal?"

"OK, deal."

"Of course, when I co-counsel, I'll have to split fees. But we both know what Solomon said 3000 years ago — and they say he was the wisest man who ever lived, the writer of Proverbs and Ecclesiastes — and he said it beautifully in Ecclesiastes 4:9 and 10, 'Two are better than one.' And then he goes on to explain *why* much better than I can.

"So Marlon, I've learned a valuable lesson through all of this. I agree with Solomon: two are better than one. I will always try to engage co-counsel on every case, no matter how little or big. I believe the results will be better and it'll be a heckava lot safer with less stress too! I may make less money, but hey, I'll have more time to be a better daddy, and money's never been my god anyway."

"OK," Marlon mumbled.

"Marlon, they've been boarding the plane and almost everyone is past the gate attendant. I'd better go, so I'll talk to you later and see you soon."

It would be no surprise. Life would be different for both of us when I returned. I hung up the greasy phone and joined the tail end of the line. After I stepped on board the plane, the attendant closed the door behind me. I found my seat, grateful for an aisle seat so I could stretch out my long legs, at least until the flight attendant came by with her rolling beverage cart.

I gave Marlon valid reasons for why I'd be co-counseling

my cases in the future, but I didn't have time enough to go into yet another reason: I didn't want to risk short-changing my clients. I would be a mediocre lawyer if I tried to handle everything myself — both criminal and civil cases — because it would then be virtually impossible NOT to drop the ball sooner or later on a client's case. All of us are human; and even with the best of intentions, we simply cannot be all things to all people, and still have the requisite expertise in very distinct and specialized areas of the law, especially when we're up against specialists in each particular area.

A lawyer who always goes it alone on his cases is either a genius and the king of multi-tasking, or he's cavalier with the lives of other people. The lone ranger type can definitely pull it off and even get awesome results, but then he's working 18 hours a day and possibly dropping the ball at home with the kids; and if that happens, he's heading down that dangerous path that leads to self-destruction, in my opinion.

I know. I lived it. My workaholism lead to mediocrity as both a lawyer and a human, at best, and under certain facts and circumstances, it was arguably reckless and even downright dangerous.

There was no way I was going to suit up as a lawyer after *all* this counseling, and still applaud mediocrity and wing it with the lives of my clients. *Excellence* was the goal from now on; and besides, the clients deserve the best. And if that means two lawyers working together making less money each, then so be it; Christ commanded us to go that extra mile. Still another bottom line: there was *no* way I was going to run the risk of being a part-time husband and daddy and not being there full swing for Elizabeth and our kids.

Chapter 31

New Life

The marathon was seemingly over. My carry on bags were finally squirreled overhead along with those of the other passengers. It was almost comical how we had politely competed for the limited room in the overhead bins, feigning concern for one another's belongings. It was kind of like the way people will compete in traffic to exit the church parking lot — even after a spirit-filled service!

"Thank you, Lord," I said aloud, after I'd squirreled my carry on bags overhead and plopped down into my aisle seat.

"You got that right!" barked the boisterous fellow in the window seat.

"They arrange these seats for the petite, or certainly not for guys like me," I joked with him.

"What about me, I'm as big as a house, but you don't see me complaining!" he bellowed once again, laughing in between swallowing and sucking on his drink.

Immediately, I felt this odd sensation that I knew him from somewhere. Then it hit me. I'd seen him earlier at the airport bar in my harried walkathon to the gate. Seated at a table that spilled out from the dark interior of the bar, this guy was all animated and yucking it up with another bar fly, pausing only long enough to imbibe more of his cocktail.

Whatever it was, there was *something* about him that had caught my attention as I maneuvered my way around the tables encroaching on the concourse. And now I felt the same feeling that I had apparently dismissed when I first saw him — envy. It had to be an envy of sorts, I figured. This guy was having fun and enjoying his drink! For a moment there, I felt like I was missing out. But then I reminded myself that I could choose to do the same thing this hero was doing any time I wanted; and instead, I'd *chosen* the healthier route. Porter and Talbott both came to mind.

And then I got all over myself for focusing on what I was *losing* or *giving up*, rather than on what I was *adding* to my life! All the Porterisms then started reverberating in my head, reminding me that *I* was the one who had reversed, so to speak, the stop and go lights in my life — it was *me* who had *chosen* to "stop" hurting and poisoning myself; and that it was *me* who had *chosen* to be kinder and gentler with myself, to *go* with the green light into a life of sobriety, a life of balance, embracing all that is good.

We often hear about someone "starting over" and having a "new life," but I was determined to actually, experientially personify these platitudes. My precious family deserved more of my attention with less distraction.

"Addictive behaviors would be given up or at least replaced," I threatened myself, as I imagined swapping out the drinking and bar hopping with healthier addictions like running and writing. (I'd have been smiling bigger at the time, had I known I'd write a couple of books and run three marathons over the next 5 years!)

I vowed to stay cognizant of the old admonition about "working to live" instead of "living to work," and to zealously guard against those insidious proclivities. "Old habits die hard," as they say, but I'd remind myself daily to *replace* the habits, somehow.

The wisdom of "the rooms" came back to me. The tapes played out in my head, repeating the words of the old black men humming about life and how we're supposed to live it. The wise men I had met in those rooms had echoed what Talbott and Porter taught — "try life as a *human being*, instead of a *human doing*."

"It ain't all about your work," I remembered one of those old black men telling me, "it's about your kin folks." Most of that meeting was about balance in our lives, I recalled, and how we needed to give more time to our relationships, especially to those at home.

"If we are not careful, we end up *doing* a million good things — instead of simply *being* a good father and a good husband and good friend to others," Pastor Dukes had told me. His sermon came back to me then and there: "It's better to 'be' than to 'do' ... and 'good' is the enemy of the 'best.' We can run around *doing* all sorts of *good* things, but this is still the enemy of the *best*, which is *being* with those we love."

The roar of the jet engines silenced my thoughts, bringing me back to the moment. Excitement came over me as the plane sped along the runway. And then that moment of exhilaration — "We're off!" I realized. We were defeating that law of gravity as the ground disappeared beneath us. The human cocktail by the window leaned back and stretched long enough for me to see a perfectly framed view of the skyscrapers of downtown Atlanta. The plane's wing dipped slightly, as if to wave goodbye. It was a fitting farewell to the city that had been my home-away-from-home for too many months.

"Take me home"

Now I was *really* on my way home! I thought of that John Denver song, "Country road, take me home ..." And then I changed the words a little while humming 'em in my head.

I imitated my drunken seat neighbor and stretched out my long legs, which protruded too far into the aisle. Then a smile graced my face as I noted my seating assignments to and from this whole Atlanta deal. They were actually symbolic of the entire journey itself. On the way up to TRC, I had been sitting in the window seat with my foggy head turned into the window pane, withdrawing from life and any action around me; and yet on the way home, I was propped in an aisle seat in the middle of life and all the action, my clear head noticing way too much.

My seat near the galley gave me an eagle eye for all that the flight attendants were up to.

A young woman caught my eye — and then I caught her eyeballing me! My flirtatious smile had been perfected over a couple of decades now, so I started to do my thing with it — but then I forced myself to look away.

Boy, that wasn't easy for me! Even though I'd broken eye contact, I was still a bit torn up with the lustful thoughts. It was really, really true, "old habits die hard." She was way too attractive, which was nothing but a sign that the *new John's* life would continue to be difficult, I reckoned.

It's just like that dirt bag enemy loser, the devil, to screw with me and my family *just* as I was flying home to greet them! But I *had* to kick his scrawny butt and win this skirmish right *here* and right *now* in the air, especially since God and the loser and I *all* knew there'd be more battles in the coming months and years on the ground.

"It is what it is," I then said aloud without realizing it, "and you just ain't playing that game anymore, pal."

"What game?" the hero next to me slurred.

"Oh, nothing," I apologized, "I was just talking to myself."

"I used to do that, too," the drunk replied, "till I started talking back!" He was howling at his own joke now, which actually was pretty funny, so I joined him. We were both laughing pretty hard.

And then it hit me! I could have fun and a lot of laughs — even with the guys who are drinking — and I can have as much fun as them and stay sober at the same time! I owed this guy for this epiphany — this revelation of sorts.

"Thanks man," I said while turning toward him, gratitude all over my face.

"For what? I didn't do jack," he slurred again, belching a

little somewhere in the middle of that remark. Then I just deflected him for a moment and left the conversation.

Reminiscing was a lot safer, so I drifted back in thought to TRC and the malling days with the boys. Smiling to myself, I remembered teasing some of the guys for the way they obsessively flirted with the mall dolls at the Lenox. But they knew what I knew — that I was only getting on them for actually acting out what I was thinking too. Before getting married, I had thrived on the whole pursuit thing, on the chase, the sport of hunting that two-legged game. But that was then; things had to be different now.

It was my stinking thinking that got me to TRC. And I wasn't about to give audience now to thoughts that would only get me into trouble. Then I recalled Proverbs 23:7, "As a man thinketh in his heart, so is he." I'd have to guard my thinking, in order to guard my heart. If I didn't guard my heart, I'd go down that slippery slope and regress to my old ways in a heartbeat.

I drew my legs back up, clearing the way for the beverage cart maneuvering in the aisle. After serving the people on the opposite side of the aisle, the flight attendant turned to me and flashed a sultry smile, asking, "What would you like, sir?" Forcing myself to focus on her makeup instead of her eyes, I answered, "Bottled water, please, and the peanuts." Then she repeated her question to my seatmate.

"This is too wild," I muttered, as the guy sitting next to me ordered a couple of cocktails, apparently one for back up in case the flight attendant took too long getting back with him.

"Please tell me I didn't look and smell like this guy before Atlanta," I silently beseeched the Father. But I suppose I wouldn't have known for sure, since clarity was quite elusive back then.

"How could I have known?" I asked myself defensively, "as the fog had only lifted when I quit indulging like 'breath of dumpster' over here — this hero sitting next to me."

Then I did a flash back to the John I was just several months earlier. "I'll have a glass of red wine," I'd habitually say in a rather robotic fashion, in response to the server's question, essentially going along to get along.

"Thank you, God," I prayed, "that I don't have to do that anymore! Thank you that I can *choose* to be healthy." I can play that tape forward in my head and see where the visual would end if I'd kept on drinking — that ugly picture! Instead of that nasty visual of a drunken husband and daddy greeting his family, I can now foresee something altogether good. I can instead choose to embrace sobriety and life and health!

"Please help this guy, Lord, to know what I now know, to choose to be kinder and gentler with himself, in Jesus' name."

"Flee!" ... But nowhere to hide!

Thankfully, the good looking flight attendant pushed the cart down the aisle and away from me. The truth of that old saying, "I can resist anything *except* temptation" teased at me a bit.

"No, you *don't*, John, change the channel!" I ordered myself. "Think about *why* this is happening. There's got to be a reason."

Maybe *Boeing* was actually created to force me to confront my demons, right here in the air, where there was no room to run and hide. This fuselage was my personal little prison — a containment of sorts, disallowing my easiest and typical method of "fleeing." I'd have to finesse other forms of 'flight."

"That's it," I figured, "God allowed *Boeing* to create these sky cylinders that trap us in space at 30,000 feet with nowhere to run, to effectuate His purpose in forcing me to deal with this curse right here and right now!" I was almost having fun teasing myself with the whole thing now.

My own little sermon was sounding off in my head as I sat there imprisoned on that plane trying to recover from that beautiful stranger in make-up, the one sporting the sky uniform.

"John, smell the coffee! Wake up and 'Flee from youthful lusts,' as He commanded you in 2 Timothy 2:22! He said it again in 1 Corinthians 6:18, John, when He said, 'Flee from sexual immorality.' So He's repeating Himself, John; and when He does that, you *know* He's absolutely serious!"

I calmed myself down a little by substituting acceptable thoughts for the unacceptable ones. I'd learned a long time ago that I couldn't just force myself to *stop thinking* about the sexual temptations. The harder I tried, the more I was focused on the very thing I was trying not to think about. I couldn't *stop* thinking about something, but I could choose to think about something *else*.

My finite mind can only hang on to one image at a time. If I tell myself to *stop* thinking about something — anything, a certain woman for example, like the one down the aisle — I'm still visualizing her as I'm telling myself *not* to. But if I choose to think of *Christ* and what He did for me on the cross, then I'm picturing *that* sacrificial love and visual in my mind. And it doesn't *have* to be Christ — it can be my kids, or anything else that's good — even a healthy questioning of the Father and His purposes or approach, not unlike what Job did.

Out of the corner of my eye, I glimpsed that sexy-looking flight attendant backing up with her cart. "Oh, *no*, *why* did I have to see that?" I thought, until I commanded myself to hunt for yet another distraction.

"Remember that verse in Job, John!" the good guy in my head reminded me. "The one that says, 'I made a covenant with my eyes not to look lustfully at a woman,' — you remember that one. Don't forget Job 31:1— or you're toast!"

Another one I tried to practice was the verse I had memorized in Atlanta, "Take captive every thought to make it obedient to Christ," 2 Corinthians 10:5. I repeated it to myself several times, but unfortunately, *I* was the one taken captive for the moment. And to break free of that bondage, I focused on the "thought life" verses, the ones in Philippians 4:8 and 9, "Whatever is right, whatever is pure, whatever is lovely," and all the other good things I was *supposed* to think about. And that *started* to help, thank God! Focusing my attention on other things — this time it was my new commitment to handle big time personal injury cases when I got home — helped me *again* to get past the lustful thoughts.

Flying High

Now that the temptation and the cart were both gone, I was stretched out again. That's when the captain made his announcement that we had reached our cruising altitude of 35,000 feet.

I did a quick calculation, rounding off the numbers. A mile is a little over 5,000 feet. At 35,000 feet, we were almost *seven miles* up in the sky! We were flying high, and so was I! I was psyched about returning to a new career focus in personal injury and wrongful death. I needed this new gig to challenge me to stay excited and passionate about my career and helping people in general. And I welcomed the opportunity to fight for what would be for me a new kind of underdog, the client oppressed by the greedy and callous insurance giants. This kind of cause was righteous, and worth getting excited about.

"Either write a check now, Sir," I told the imaginary adjuster in my head, "or we'll have a jury tell you to write a bigger one later, to include punitive damages and attorney's fees." I spent the next few minutes in that world of civil litigation, psyching myself up for the future.

Truth be told, I was also pretty pumped about my small victories on the plane. I'd said *no* to the alcohol and *no* to the pursuit of women. There were times when I'd lay on my uncomfortable mattress at TRC, unable to sleep because of my roommate's snoring. "How am I going to handle annoying and irritating things like this once I leave this safe environment at

TRC?" I'd often wonder. We *had* to handle these things at TRC without the benefit of taking the edge off with a little wine; but what about after I left?

It was a small test, but I'd passed it with flying colors! I held aloft my little plastic bottle of water as a salute to this first small victory. Then, in an almost unconscious manner, I repeated the motion as I saluted my victory in declining to play games with the flight attendant — the same fine looking woman who'd handed me the same water bottle I now held aloft.

These were victories, to be sure, and yet I knew stronger temptations lay ahead. I couldn't let my guard down because of these two small victories. "Be careful John," I said almost aloud, "you can't fly this high all the time — there'll be all sorts of bumps in the air in this turbulent thing we call 'life,' and plummeting lows are sure to be expected."

Sober thoughts were creeping into my private little emotional high, and I welcomed the self talk as a necessary tutor. "Soon enough we'll be on the ground," I reminded the other guy in my head, "and it's then that you need to STAY grounded!"

Chapter 32

Journey Home

Then it dawned on me, as the flight attendant cruised along with the cart, that nothing in the plane was bouncing around; this flight was smoother than most. And then I flashed back to the flight I had experienced on the way up to TRC. The flight up was filled with turbulence, including several sharp drops in altitude.

"Hey, watch my drink will ya, so she don't take it!" My window-seat-neighbor slobbered at me, as he hacked and coughed his way past me for the restroom.

"Sure," I replied, just before silently adding, "Anything else you need?" I shifted my legs to the side as he poured himself into the aisle and staggered away.

But then I got to thinking, what a markedly different flight *this* one was becoming, as compared to the flight up. It was now calm and peaceful, at least since I scored these mini-victories. My new and calmer spirit was a gift as much as it was a relief. And *I* was so much easier to live with now.

Months earlier on the plane to TRC, I was in the clouds in more ways than one — I'd struggled with the turbulence in my soul, nursing a very defeated spirit. But for the moment anyway, it was all clear and sunny skies. I was flying auto pilot now, in more ways than one.

And this was a markedly different flight, in more ways than one. On the way up to Atlanta, I traveled *with* Elizabeth. On this flight, I'm traveling home *to* Elizabeth.

Eager to connect with Elizabeth, I opened my briefcase and took out the little book, *The Prayer of Jabez*, which she had mailed to me as a gift. Elizabeth had written this encouraging, sweet message on the inside cover of the book:

My Dearest John:

I believe the "best" is yet to come!! I feel it deep down within. God is so ready to pour out His blessings upon you abundantly!!

Enjoy this book ... I'll be reading it here — while you are reading it there. God is faithful and He loves you, John, very, very much ...

(Elizabeth wrote some other sweet words that are omitted here.)

I would often read this handwritten note when I was in Atlanta, whenever I felt like boosting myself with encouragement. She wasn't with me on the flight back, but her words were. I wasn't alone at all. My God was with me — in Spirit and in every other sense — and so was Elizabeth.

Reading her beautiful, heartfelt words of encouragement in that little book moved me to retrieve and re-read the letter I'd written to her in response:

I love you, Sweetheart, and I thank God for you too. You've kept our family together without any help from me the whole time I've been away, and that could not have been easy. He blessed me with a wonderful, sweet and precious wife, and this I know. I've read and re-read your very sweet and loving words of encouragement in the book, "The Prayer of Jabez," and I now agree with you, Honey, "The best is yet to come!"

I'll make it up to you, Baby, I promise. Thank you for being the awesome wife you are, and the world's best mother! Our 3 extraordinarily awesome kids are blessed big time to have a Mommy like you!

I love you and I miss you too. We'll do some fun stuff when we're together again, OK? We'll

take some alone time and go away for some
weekends to NYC and Georgetown, DC, and
we'll take some fun family vacations too, OK?
I love you, Sweetheart, big time! And I can't
wait to see you at home!
Love, John

I was moved then and there to read and reread the letters
that I had mailed to my children a month earlier. They were
written late one night when I was in my apartment at TRC
missing my kids terribly. I kept copies of the letters in my
Bible as a constant reminder to follow through on my
promises to each of them. Though I'd be with the kids in an
hour or so, I was missing them like I was still in Atlanta.
Rereading my promises on the plane made me even more
committed to keeping them.

Just as I'd promised Elizabeth that we'd spend some special
time together doing what she'd enjoy, I wanted each of my
children to know that I wanted to do something special with
them. We all know that kids spell L.O.V.E., T.I.M.E. And that
meant time spent with their Daddy.

To our ten-year-old daughter, I wrote:

Kathleenchan, I miss you big time,
Sweetheart! You are the most wonderful girly in
the whole world — my angel girl!

I cannot wait to be with you again,
permanently! I'm so proud of you! You and I
will take the red car to the mall and do some
shopping, and we'll get your hair cut the way
you love it. And all of us will go camping and
do all kinds of cool, fun things, OK? I love you
Kathleenchan! Love, Daddy

To our nine-year-old son, I wrote:

> *Johnny, you are Daddy's personal hero! You are getting so big and more special all the time. Thank you for being there for your Mommy and your sisters — you've done a great job!*
>
> *I can't wait to be with you. Let's spend a lot of time together when I return, OK? We'll go to a Marlin's game and we're going to have a great time together doing cool things! I love you Johnny, more than life itself! Love, Daddy, your biggest fan!*

To our four-year-old daughter, I wrote:

> *I miss you soooo much, Marychan! You're Daddy's girl, the sweetest girly girl in the whole wide world, you know that? Big hugs and kisses when I see you, OK?*
>
> *We'll be together again soon and we're going to have so much fun, so get ready! We'll go to the Metrozoo and do lots of other fun things too. I love you, Marychan! Love, Daddy*

I finished reading the letters just as I heard the pilot.

"Ladies and gentlemen, we are beginning our final descent into the Fort Lauderdale — Hollywood International airport."

I put away my things and returned my seat to its full upright position, just as the guy by the window woke up from his stupor.

"Hey, you from here?" he managed to ask. As I was nodding in the affirmative, he continued, "What bars do you recommend in this city?"

"None, though I once closed 'em all. I would recommend a taxi, though, and then some sleep, as that could be a good thing, whadayathink?"

"I think you're a jerk," he slurred.

"I've been told that … so maybe I'll have to take a look at that," I replied, hoping to deescalate things.

"You do that."

"Father, please help this guy," I asked, as I then looked past him and out the window to see the signs of actual civilization. And thankfully, there they were — the familiar highways and buildings, so I knew we were close!

I knew we were almost ready for touchdown when the nose of the plane angled up slightly. Then, a small bump and I was home!

Reading the letters had me in a good mental and emotional place when we taxied up to the arrival gate. The pilot interrupted my thoughts once again. "Please be careful when opening the overhead bins as items may have shifted during the flight …"

It was then at that otherwise insignificant moment that I vividly recall deciding to forgive myself — again, on a deeper level — for the old days.

Between all the letters I'd read on the plane, I had just enough encouragement to resurrect everything else I had learned, "processed" and relearned in Atlanta. I was ready for my new life; I was ready to come home.

…

"Daddy!! Daddy!!" They shouted, almost in unison. The rest of the terminal was a blur.

Kathleen, Johnny and Mary, the three most precious children on the planet — "I *never* want to be away from you again, *ever*!" I yelled in my head, my heart racing as fast as my feet toward them. We embraced almost mid air, while I let go of my tears of joy. I don't know that I've ever hugged anyone longer or harder than I did that day. Each of them could've seen a chiropractor when I was done with them!

Elizabeth was smiling and watching from a few feet away.

Then it was our turn. She looked as beautiful and sweet as the day I first saw her. Our kids watched us embrace. We were both more relaxed — essentially *relieved* it was over, stealing a glance at the kids who were smiling ear to ear.

"It's so good to have you home, John," Elizabeth said, sounding as sensitive as ever. "You look great." We talked for a while as the kids ran ahead of us a little. After sharing some good updates and a few more personal, loving, warm and fuzzy comments, she asked, "How are you feeling?"

"Fine," is all I started to say. But then I recalled what they taught me at TRC, "If anyone asks you how you feel and you say 'fine,' don't forget that 'fine' means 'fake, insecure, neurotic and emotionally-dishonest.'"

So then I followed up with a more emotionally-honest answer:

"I'm glad to be home, Sweetheart, but at the same time, I'm concerned about my business and my ability to provide for you guys; and I'm not exactly psyched about facing a lot of my friends around the courthouse asking me, 'Where you been?'"

Elizabeth replied, "They'll just think you were on vacation. And from the tan you have, it looks that way."

Smiling, I knew she was right. "You know, Honey, life will be a little more boring from now on," I teased Elizabeth.

"Hey, I'll take boring anytime over whatever *that* was!" Elizabeth responded, playfully punching me in the arm and laughing for a change.

"Yes, this is better," I told myself, "and much safer, too," as I internally affirmed my earlier decision to focus on Elizabeth and the kids and keep doing the next right thing. God had given me this wonderful family to love — this incredible hand to play. And who knows, if I played this hand the right way — His way — it just might be anything but boring!

It's good to be home, thank God.

Epilogue

It has been over six years since I returned from TRC, and life is better. My family is well adjusted, and everyone is healthy and doing well, thank God. Our world is less eventful, but that's a good thing. Instead of taking the edge off with a couple glasses of wine most nights, I'll run an hour along the beach before court or on the roads around our hometown; the effect is the same — a more relaxed, peaceful feeling that envelops me, and consequently the people around me.

I've written a couple of books and run a few marathons since the Atlanta days, no doubt as a result of all the renewed energy born of a healthier lifestyle. It hasn't been six years of total abstinence and sobriety. I went for about four years without indulging at all, but then I experimented, flirting with relapse and even disaster.

The good news: the obsession was lifted, thank God, and I don't need to do it. I'll still occasionally have a glass or two of wine, but that's the key — "occasionally." And when I do, I'm smart enough to be with my wife and to create healthier boundaries. Most of the time, I'll play that tape out in my mind and see how the movie ends (i.e., imagining my disappointment and remorse the next day, and visualizing what stupid things I might have done while drinking); and then I'll use the wisdom God gave me to decide not to even go there.

My gratitude list keeps growing; His blessings are immeasurable, counting all the little ones we take for granted: every breath we take, every heartbeat, food and shelter, the life and health of our children and other loved ones, the smiles we receive each day from friends and strangers alike, a random kind word, and the list goes on and on.

Life is less wild, and that's a good thing.

About the Author

"John Contini is one of the most brilliant men that I have met. He is a gifted lawyer and has a unique gift of leadership, especially in the courtroom. John is a dear friend and a man of great stature in the community."

Senior Pastor Dino Pedrone
New Testament Baptist Church
Miami Lakes, Florida

"John will wear you out in trial. As a prosecutor trying a case with him, I am often frustrated because he is such a good attorney. It is almost as if John knows what I am going to say before I say it and then diffuses it. He will pick apart the big points in my case. John is relentless, and he often takes the 'wind out the sails' for the prosecution.

"For the past 19 years, I have prosecuted homicide cases — over 80 trials — so I have had cases with most of the best lawyers in South Florida. John is different than other criminal defense lawyers because of his strong convictions. John really believes in people, and he genuinely cares about his clients."

Brian Cavanagh
Assistant State Attorney/prosecutor
Chief of Homicide
Broward State Attorney's Office

"I was a Fort Lauderdale police officer in the organized crime division before I went to law school in 1981. My law enforcement background makes me a better attorney and a better person. Most days I enjoy my work, because I know how the system can chew people up if they are not represented by a disciplined and conscientious lawyer.

"John and I met in 1984 when we were both prosecutors for the state attorney's office in Broward County. John and I were friends even back then, though he was a single wild guy and I had a wife and three young kids ... so our career paths and personal paths were different at that time."

Mike Dutko
criminal defense lawyer

"Hard-charging people like John are naturally drawn to the world of criminal law. We are the old-time gladiators who revel in a good fight, so criminal law attracts us.

"I admire John for making the positive changes that are now evident to those of us who know him. John recovered well, and 'recoverers' are better lawyers, because they have strong moral structure. The principles in the 12 Steps are for *everyone*, not just for people who *choose* to be in recovery. What hurts the lawyer is the need to be in recovery and choosing not to go. If *everyone* went to a rehab — and everyone *needs* to for *something* — this world would be a far better place."

Howard Finkelstein
Broward County Public Defender
WSVN/TV 7's *Help Me Howard*
Television Segment

"John and I have been friends for years. I saw that he was on a path that could ruin his career and his life. John is an emotional man with a relentless spirit, who really cares about the people he represents. Since he returned from Atlanta, he is more open, more forthcoming and more candid. It is easy now for me to be close to John.

"Most people in recovery are good people who dealt with their problems in a bad way. Many of them — due to their addictions — lost their families, their jobs, their friends and their self-respect, before they surrendered to win."

Judge Robert Fogan
Senior Circuit Court Judge
Broward County

"As a police officer, I knew John Contini from his early days as a prosecutor and all the selfless help he provided to me back then. He gave a lot of his time and energy to help the police specifically on cases in which we were trying to get to the pimps involved with the prostitution of young girls on Fort Lauderdale beach. John struck me as being very respectful and compassionate to everyone involved.

"I became friends with John when he was a prosecutor; and when he became a criminal defense lawyer, we remained friends. Even though we ended up on opposite sides, we each had a job to do; and we respected what the other was doing. John is a hard worker who puts in long hours. He works weekends and nights and does whatever it takes to get the job done properly."

Detective Sergeant Frank Miller
Fort Lauderdale Police Department

"John is one of the most compassionate men I have ever met. While earning the reputation as one of the nation's top criminal defense lawyers, John is forever looking for the redemptive opportunity in each person he meets or serves. The story most exemplifying the true character of John is the story regarding the time a young man broke into our home. I enlisted John's help to see what we could do to help this young man. John's intervention not only kept the young man out of jail but John also paid his way to take a taxi to church for five Sundays in a row.

"I have had the privilege of serving as John's pastor and friend for the past eleven years. There is not another man like John Contini. He would give the shirt off his back to help his fellow man. His passion for the Savior he serves is an inspiration to all who have the privilege of meeting him. He loves his family and has one of the godliest wives I have met. His children follow the example of their parents and love the Lord and faithfully serve Him."

Dr. Larry L. Thompson
Senior Pastor
First Baptist Church
Fort Lauderdale, Florida

"John Contini is an example to which others should aspire. The majority of defense attorneys are more concerned about the law and winning the case than about the welfare of their client. John is different. He displays a concern for the individual. He addresses the underlying problem that has created the trouble for the client in the first place so that hopefully it doesn't happen again."

Judge Steven Deluca
County Court Judge
Broward County
Fort Lauderdale, Florida

"John epitomizes professionalism, and he's an example that there's nothing inconsistent with being a gentleman and being a very effective lawyer."

Judge Fred Horowitz
Circuit Court Judge
Broward County
Fort Lauderdale, Florida

"John Contini has a reputation as a good man and a good lawyer."

Judge Stanton Kaplan
Circuit Court Judge
Broward County
Fort Lauderdale, Florida

"John is a very loyal and compassionate attorney who generally goes beyond what is expected. He makes it a personal thing. He becomes very compassionate and he's always looking out for his client's welfare — even if he knew the person committed the crime. The difference between John and other attorneys is that most attorneys treat it like a job. John doesn't. John treats everyone with a tremendous amount of respect. John always looks at the good in a person."

Frank Carbone
polygraphist
former President of the
Florida Polygraph Association

About the Author's Background:

John Contini was born in Cleveland, Ohio, and went to high school, college and law school in Boston, Massachusetts. He received his B.A. in 1979 from the University of Massachusetts and his Juris Doctor in 1982 from the New England School of Law.

In 1983, John moved to Florida and began his legal career as an Assistant State Attorney — known on the street as a prosecutor — working from 1983-1987 in the Broward County State Attorney's Office. In 1985, he was chosen from a field of over 100 prosecutors within the office to head the Obscenity Unit, responsible for prosecuting those accused of obscenity-related crimes in strip clubs, swingers' clubs, adult movie theatres and adult book stores.

John became a criminal defense attorney in 1987, developing a reputation as a lawyer willing to defend the indefensible. He was renowned as a defense lawyer for his defense of those charged with first degree murder facing the electric chair. Then he moved beyond the local scene to defend the criminally accused in federal courts throughout the nation. John has defended indicted individuals against prosecutions in Fort Worth, Texas, Trenton, New Jersey, Pittsburgh, Pennsylvania, Boston, Massachusetts, Cleveland, Ohio, and closer to home, Orlando, Fort Lauderdale and Miami, Florida.

In 2001, John expanded his legal practice to also focus on personal injury and wrongful death cases. Among other professional associations, John is a member of the Florida Bar, the Federal Trial Bar, the Massachusetts Bar, the National Association of Criminal Defense Lawyers, and the Association of Trial Lawyers of America.

A Christian since 1991, John deftly intertwines his beliefs with his professional experience. He believes that being a good lawyer is not just about winning and it's not just about caring for people — it's about both. As an extension of his faith, he speaks at area schools, drug and alcohol rehabilitation facilities, jails and prisons, juvenile boot camps and church youth groups. He also has had many spirited debates with opposing lawyers on radio and TV talk shows. In spite of all these demands on his time, he's also a committed family man. His wife, Elizabeth, and their three children, Kathleen, Johnny and Mary, are at the center of his life.

About the Author's Family, 2007:

Elizabeth, my wife, is a beautiful person, not only in her appearance, but in her spirit.

Those who meet Elizabeth immediately recognize how quintessentially sweet and genuine she is, and those who really get to know Elizabeth, truly love her. She lights up a room with her bright smile, happy spirit and tremendous energy. She is bubbly, honest, and has a great sense of humor.

After being home-schooled for years, our children attended a Christian school, where the school President honored Elizabeth with a post on their Board of Directors. Later Elizabeth became a teacher at another Christian school, where she earned the respect and affections of all the students, parents and faculty. While simultaneously teaching and raising our children, she finished her college education part time in the evenings, earning a 4.0 grade point average while at Trinity International University.

God worked through Elizabeth to impact and reach her husband — and therefore our children — for the Kingdom. Her unwavering commitment to her faith has been the greatest example and evidence of the truth of the gospel that I have seen.

Kathleen is now 17. I am so proud to be her Daddy. She is absolutely stunning — radiating beauty — while personifying the more important qualities of compassion, grace and sweetness. She will not only turn your head; she will touch your heart.

Kathleen is as sensitive as she is intuitive — an old soul at a very young age. God has blessed her with real perception, intuition and wisdom beyond her years. Everyone who gets to know Kathleen appears to adore her. She genuinely enjoys helping people. Her friends confide in her, as she has earned a reputation for keeping their confidences.

Kathleen Yoshiko Contini, my first born, was used mightily by God to change my life. I love my Kathleenchan, as I affectionately call her, more than life itself. I'm her #1 fan — and always will be — right up there alongside her mother, no doubt. A hug from my daughter improves my life and melts my heart, making *everything* worthwhile.

Johnny is now 16. He is as sweet-spirited and kind as he is strong and athletic; and he is as handsome as he is funny and bright. It is apparent that God had a good reason when He saved Johnny from an early childhood near-death experience. He is an exceptional person and a blessing to everyone he meets. Johnny makes friends very easily, whether at school, church or in the community.

Johnny has been selected to participate in the "Honor's Choir," a highly coveted position among the students at the Christian school he attends in Fort Lauderdale. He has also been very active in school sports, including track, wrestling and now high school varsity football. His student peers and teachers honored Johnny with the prestigious "Barnabas Award," bestowed upon *one* student in his grade for encouraging those around him.

Most importantly, my son, Johnnychan, as I affectionately call him, has made me a better man. His example of integrity at such an early age impacted me before the Father. He is my personal hero. No father could be prouder than I am to have Johnny as my boy; and no father could love a son more than I love Johnny Patrick Kyoshi Contini.

Mary is now 11. She is the most vibrant and sweet-spirited young girl on the planet, thank God. Her beauty is arguably surpassed only by her sensitivity, kindness and intelligence. Mary has rarely achieved less than an "A" in school, and yet her accomplishments are not limited to academics. She was awarded the coveted "Master's Award" for "Most Christ-like Character."

Singled out among all the boys and girls in her grade, Mary received the "Outstanding Athlete Award." She is a blessing to her many friends at school, church and dance, who appear to be drawn to Mary by her genuineness, gentleness, and sweetness.

Marychan makes my heart smile. She adds tremendous joy to my life, and she has blessed my days beyond imagination. Mary is extraordinarily sensitive to the feelings and needs of others, including me. Her affectionate hugs for daddy are more than priceless. I love this little girl — as I do my other children — more than words can possibly describe, and I thank God repeatedly for Mary Elizabeth McBride Kyo Contini.

About Uncle Rocco:

Elizabeth's words:
Uncle Rocco came to our kids' activities, regardless of how uneventful the ballet recital or school play might be. By coming, he was making a statement that you and your children were important to him. He was very generous. He loved us and we knew it.

John's words:
My uncle, Rocco Contini, loved to learn things, and part of his daily routine included a trip to Barnes & Noble. He knew how to teach himself things — golfing, motor homes, the computer, the stock market — whatever he was interested in. He taught himself about boating when he owned a boat, about horses when he owned horses, and about the restaurant business when he owned a restaurant.

When I worked at his restaurant, he gave me respect but expected excellence. He didn't just delegate and give orders; he'd show me how to do it first. Then he'd work with me, like when he stood beside me getting his hands messy with salad dressing. He loved to learn and to teach others what he'd learned, like when he taught my kids how to play pool.

Uncle Rocco was a good athlete. Even as an older man, he was still walking three miles a day. As a kid, they called him "Toughy," because he was an incredibly tough football player. However, he gave up both football and school to support the family when his father died young. As a boy, Rocco worked a man's job in a brick yard.

He became an absolutely fearless entrepreneur, full of life and confidence. He started a gas station, became president of the *Broward County Bowler's Association*, and started his own highly successful insurance agency — *Contini Insurance*, earning awards year after year as a "million dollar round table member." He started a restaurant, *The Fishhouse Five*. And he started a bookstore with his daughter, Diana, *The Book Emporium*.

He came from no money, and yet he saved a small fortune, just so he could give it away to family. My uncle helped everyone in the family. He helped my Dad as a brother and a best friend. When I thought I was in trouble years ago, he helped me explain the situation to my Dad.

When I once spoke disrespectfully to my Uncle Roc in my home, he left my house. I called him the next day for lunch, to apologize and ask him for his forgiveness. He forgave me immediately, and he never lectured me; he loved me just as much as before. He was the kind of guy who would not only forgive, but he'd forget; just like Jeremiah 31:34 tells us that when God forgives, He forgets.

Uncle Roc not only told me that he was a believer, he acted out his beliefs. He sent me e-mails about our Faith, he attended our Christmas pageant every year, and at times he prayed with me. His entire countenance would change markedly whenever we would pray together. One time after I prayed for him, he said: "Thank you, thank you, thank you." But now I say, "Thank *you*, Uncle Roc!"

About the Author's first book, *Danger Road*:

Danger Road is the incredible true story of three drug dealers who were brutally murdered in 1983 on Danger Road in the Florida Everglades. Lured into a phony drug deal each victim hoped would be his big retirement score, they allegedly found themselves at the business end of a gun wielded by a Miami-Dade police officer. But police and prosecutors say Officer Gilbert Fernandez Jr. and his cohorts weren't there to arrest the drug dealers. They were there to kill them and steal their nine kilos of cocaine.

Danger Road details the transformation of Fernandez, a former Mr. Florida bodybuilding champion and black belt in karate, who became a Christian during the intervening years between the 1983 murders and his subsequent arrest in 1990.

This was no courthouse conversion. The man who was once named "Miami's Meanest Cop" had been a Christian for several years by the time of his trial. He no longer abused and intimidated detainees and others he came into contact with. And he no longer managed the violent ring of bodybuilder-debt collectors out of the notorious Apollo Gym, which he eventually owned. Now he lived to convert people at his gym to faith in Jesus Christ.

But in 1991 Fernandez found himself on trial for his life.

Does God give second chances? In *Danger Road* you'll discover why He's called the "God of the Second Chance."

Danger Road Reviews:

DANGER ROAD rips the curtain off a high profile murder case that has the highest stakes possible: life or death. Then it takes you into the bowels of the justice system and on this journey you go from the darkest, coldest heart to the crowning glory of the human condition. DANGER ROAD is a searing and scintillating gawk at the truth about our legal system and ourselves.

John Contini proves that when you fight monsters you don't have to become a monster...you can become a man of God.

Howard Finkelstein
Broward County Public Defender
Help Me Howard Television Segment

John's work goes beyond just being another "true crime" book: It is a riveting morality treatise affording extraordinary insight into a homicide's rippling effects not only on the immediate participants, but on all who are touched by the ongoing waves of its horror — yet revealing hope that a measure of good can spring out of even the machinations of evil.

Brian Cavanagh
Chief of Homicide
Office of the Broward State Attorney

DANGER ROAD by John Contini is a great work of art which provides insight into the trial of a death penalty case.

Every lawyer and judge should obtain a copy of this brilliant book by a veteran attorney.

Alan H. Schreiber
The elected Public Defender
of Broward County from 1976-2004

About the Author, prior to release of *Danger Road*:

Article by Jo Urbanovitch

Used with permission of Jo Urbanovitch, WDC Media

Criminal Attorney Sees Need for Forgiveness, Mercy, in Court — and in Life

FORT LAUDERDALE (February 22, 2006) — John Contini knows first-hand what it's like to walk in another man's shoes. A criminal lawyer and deeply spiritual man, he's been striving for 23 years to find a healthy balance, a way to serve justice in a secularized criminal legal system — an arena with practices juxtaposed to his own personal belief in the necessity for compassion, mercy, and forgiveness. Somehow he has been able to bridge these seemingly irreconcilable worlds.

"You've got to do certain things to win in trial, and represent your client to the very best of your ability — legal practices that are ethically permitted by the rules of evidence and actually ethically required by the Code of Professional Responsibility — but behavior that can occasionally run afoul of the scriptures," explained the high-profile criminal defense and personal injury lawyer. "It's like tip-toeing through an ethical and scriptural minefield."

Though most of Contini's cases are in South Florida, he has handled federal cases involving corporate espionage, organized crime and racketeering, smuggling, and drug trafficking — and other crimes — in various U.S. locales like Pittsburgh, Boston, Cleveland, Ohio and Orlando, Florida. Contini, who lives in Fort Lauderdale, has a reputation as one of the most capable and successful defense attorneys in America.

His personal and professional journey has taken him from the depths of emotional despair over the state of an unforgiving world, and the weakness and hypocrisy inherent in human nature, to the pinnacle of spiritual joy and fulfillment. The challenges he has faced, and their resolutions — from both a legal and spiritual position — have enabled him to grow and flourish as a lawyer, and as a man. Working side by side with those who have been truly repentant, Contini has had to struggle with his own ego and personal demons, witnessing the astonishing duality that lies within the hearts of his dear friends, respected peers, and those he has represented.

Though most people may be totally comfortable with the meting out of punishment to any and all members of society (as long as it's not someone they love), Contini is more interested in finding ways to be compassionate in his practice.

Contini is quick to point out that being compassionate does not mean setting a convicted killer or pedophile free. He believes that criminals can be forgiven, and still go to prison where, he says, most deserve to be.

"Many of the angry, self-righteous folks, who clamor for the accused to be put to death or sent to prison for life, are the very same people who would ask for mercy if it were their father, mother, big brother, elder sister, prodigal son, or wayward daughter who had done the deed," noted Contini. "People want justice when someone else is accused. They want anything but justice when a loved one is on trial. Then they demand mercy, and suddenly want to be assured that their loved one will get the help they so desperately need. They talk out of both corners of their mouth. We simply need to acknowledge there's value in trying to avoid this kind of double-mindedness."

Ironically, much of what Contini has learned about life, his own failings and weaknesses, and his blossoming spirituality, was gleaned from relationships with some of his most infamous and notorious clients. His close contact with Gil Fernandez, the former Miami police officer and champion bodybuilder who was convicted of the triple gangland-style murder of three alleged drug dealers in 1991, helped to change Contini's life.

"I got too close to Gil, and probably should have tried harder to maintain appropriate boundaries, and put a healthy distance between myself and my client," he said. "But I don't regret a thing. Now after 20 years as a criminal defense lawyer, I only take clients who I believe are truly repentant — those who show remorse for their crime, and empathy for the victim and the victim's family. As a man of faith, my relationship with Gil helped me to practice what I used to just preach."

In his soon-to-be-released book on the case, *Danger Road: A True Crime Story of Murder and Redemption*, Contini recounts the incredible story of his complicated relationship with Fernandez. Now a lifelong bond, their relationship developed around the nine-week trial in which Contini defended Fernandez, and culminated in a spiritual awakening for both the attorney and the convicted man.

"The biggest challenge I face as a lawyer, and a man of faith in this secular arena, is simply acting in a way that is consistent with all of who I am," said Contini. "It can be very difficult when you want to forcefully tell a pompous and uncaring prosecutor to back off. Instead, I try to get people to realize that we all have something to learn from each other — even a person who is a convicted murderer has some kind of wisdom to share. There but for the grace of God go I."

Regardless of a person's guilt, whether in reference to Gil Fernandez or any other person who has been accused of a heinous crime, Contini believes that if you know the defendant is guilty, it's crucial to "condemn the act, not the person."

"The criminally accused is treated as our modern-day leper," explained Contini. "It's not the healthy who need a physician. It's the person who is shunned and ostracized by society who we ought to help, and treat with compassion and mercy. After all, we must demonstrate forgiveness if we want to be forgiven for the mistakes we have made in this life."

"In this world you will have trouble."

All of us will have trouble in this world from time to time, and on this fact we can all agree; however, Jesus tells us in John 16:33, "In this world you will have trouble, but take heart, I have overcome the world." (emphasis added) Notice that He did not say that we *might* have trouble in this world, but instead, He specifically told us that we *will* have trouble. It's almost comforting to know that He absolutely assured us of the fact that we will have these troubles, inasmuch as we can then expect that the troubles will come, we won't be shocked when they do occur, and we can hopefully then resist the otherwise natural tendency to internalize our troubles, erroneously believing that we are somehow so markedly different from other people, or beyond hope.

Yes, the fact that we are assured by Christ that we will have trouble, is almost good news, as crazy or wild as that sounds. The really good news, however, is the very real, additional fact that He is always right there with us to help us through these troubles. He promised, "I am with you wherever you will go. I will never leave you or forsake you." (Deut. 31:6; Heb. 13:5) ... "I am with you always, even to the end of the age." (Matthew 28:20) ... He also promised that He would always live to make intercession for us, and that He will even pray for us when we don't know how we ought to pray, or what words we ought to use. (Rom. 8:26) Now how can all of this not be great news? Not only did He die for our sins and then resurrect to give us power over death and the enemy, but He even stays with us through all of our trouble and helps us beat the problems we face, all the while even praying for us too! Can you imagine that some folks still choose to reject this free gift, a gift that costs us nothing, while it cost Him everything.

Photo Gallery

With my Uncle Rocco, before Atlanta

My kids, by our Christmas tree, months before Atlanta; the photo I had at TRC

Dr. Doug Talbott

Talbott Recovery Campus
Atlanta, Georgia

Pastor Jerome Dukes
Community Fellowship Christian Church
International.

Community Fellowship Christian Church
International.

Pastor Larry Thompson
First Baptist Church of downtown Fort Lauderdale,

Broward County Judge
Robert Fogan

Broward County Judge
Paul Backman

Mike Dutko

Howard Finkelstein
Broward County Public Defender
Help Me Howard television segment and
Legal Expert, WSVN-7 Miami

Brian Cavanagh

My state attorney badge

*My kids crossing the finish line
(they jumped the fence at the 26 mile mark),
finishing the last .2 miles with me;
Palm Beach Marathon, after Atlanta*

*Four marathons and two books later;
healthier days!*